A SOURCE-BOOK OF
MODERN HINDUISM

Edited by

GLYN RICHARDS

CURZON PRESS

First published 1985
Curzon Press Ltd : London and Dublin

© Glyn Richards 1985

British Library Cataloguing in Publication Data
A Source-book of modern Hinduism
1. Hinduism — History
I. Richards, Glyn
294.5'09'034   BL1150
ISBN 0 7007 0173 7

Printed and bound in Great Britain by
Biddles Ltd, Guildford and King's Lynn

For Hywel, Ann, Geraint and Helen

CONTENTS

PREFACE

I have attempted in this volume to compile selections from the works of modern Hindu writers who may be considered to be inheritors of the religious and social traditions of India and who have made an important contribution to the renaissance of Hinduism and the reformation of Indian society. The selection does not claim to be exhaustive in any way but the writers chosen would generally be regarded as leaders of thought in nineteenth and twentieth century India and their views of significance in the development of modern India. The themes which have determined the choice of texts are in the main those relating to religion, social and economic reforms, education and politics. The selection from each writer is preceded by brief biographical details and an assessment of his contribution to Indian society.

I am indebted to the staff of the inter-library loan department of the University of Stirling for their unfailing courtesy and generous help in securing for me a number of the books required for the compilation of this volume; to the staff of the Centre of South Asian Studies at the University of Cambridge for their prompt response to my inquiries and their readiness to photocopy selections from one of the books in their library; to my colleague John Riddy for an extract from one of the letters in the MacNabb archives at Killin, Tayside; and to Mrs Linda Greig for her cheerful co-operation and expert assistance in typing the manuscript. A word of thanks is also due to my students over the years in the course on Modern Hinduism who have shown me the need for a volume of this sort and to my wife for her assistance in preparing the book for the publisher.

I wish to express my appreciation to the following publishers for permission to include in this volume selections from their publications: Oxford University Press for selections from S. Radhakrishnan, *Eastern Religions and Western Thought*; George Allen and Unwin for selections from S. Radhakrishnan, *An Idealist View of Life, The Hindu View of Life, Religion in a Changing World*, and from Rabindranath Tagore, *The Religion of Man*; Macmillan for selections from Rabindranath Tagore, *Personality: Lectures delivered in America*; and *Gitanjali (Song Offerings)*; Sri Aurobindo Ashram, Pondicherry, for selections from Aurobindo Ghose, *The Life Divine, On Himself, The*

Human Cycle, The Ideal of Unity, War and Self-Determination, and *The Synthesis of Yoga*; Vision Books, New Delhi, for selections from S. Radhakrishnan, *Indian Religions*; Navajivan Trust, Ahmedabad, for selections from *The Selected Works of Mahatma Gandhi*, and Nimal Kumar Bose, *Selections from Gandhi*; Sevagram Ashram Pratishtan, Wardha, for selections from Vinoba Bhave, *Democratic Values and the Practice of Citizenship*, and *Thoughts on Education*.

In the extracts which follow, the original spelling and style have been retained. This accounts for occasional variations in rendering the same words and for some inconsistencies in punctuation, even within selections from the same author.

GLYN RICHARDS

1

RĀMMOHAN ROY (1772 – 1833)

Rāmmohan Roy has been described as the father of modern India and one of the greatest benefactors of mankind. However difficult the task of making an objective assessment of his role in the renaissance of Hinduism and the modernization of India may be the fact that he made a significant contribution to the reformation of Hindu society and religion is not in question.

He was born in 1772 into an orthodox Hindu family of Brahmins who were engaged in revenue farming under the aegis of the East India Company. Whatever the doubts about his early education at Patna and Benares it is clear that he had a close association with Muslim scholars and under their guidance became well acquainted with Arabic and Persian philosophic literature. At the age of 16 he is reputed to have written a paper questioning the idolatry of the Hindu system and expressing an aversion to British power in India. This aversion, if authentic, must have been overcome during his years of travel throughout India and beyond because on his return home he entered the Bengal Civil Service in the employment of the British. His business acumen and success as an administrator enabled him to accumulate sufficient capital and secure enough income from estates he had purchased to retire. By 1815 he had settled in Calcutta and had begun to devote his time and energy to the task of religious and social reform. He considered religion and politics to be interrelated and believed some change in the Hindu religious system to be necessary if only to secure political and social advantage for the Hindus.

His enthusiasm for reform may be traced in part to Hindu and Islamic thought, including Vedāntic philosophy and Muslim theology, and partly to Western ideas including Unitarian doctrines and eighteenth-century European deism. In the religious sphere his reforming zeal took the form of a rejection of image worship as indicative of prejudice and superstition and contrary to reason and common sense. His *Vedānta grantha*, a Bengali translation of the Vedānta, sought to establish the unity and supremacy of Brahman as Eternal Being and his work on the

Upanishads propounded the idea of nirguṇa Brahman as one without a second. Image worship, in his view, was worship of an inferior kind and Hindus like other people throughout the world should worship without the aid of images. Equally erroneous were the dietary laws of Hinduism violation of which resulted in more severe penalties than theft or murder. While the latter produced judicial sentences and could be expiated by religious ceremonies and gifts to Brāhmin priests, the former were punished by loss of caste and separation from family and friends.

He rejected also the violation of human rights perpetrated in the name of religion involving sati, the burning of widows on the funeral pyres of their husbands. The violent death to which the unfortunate females of India, particularly Bengal, were being subjected was both inhuman and morally indefensible and could only lead to the moral debasement of those who condoned the practice.

In his attempt to enlighten his fellow countrymen Roy promoted journalism, editing newspapers and periodicals in English, Persian (*Mirat-ul-Ukhbar*) and Bengali (*Sambad Kaumadi*), brought out Bengali translations of the shastras, and supported Bengali versions of English scientific and literary texts. His stress on the importance of the vernacular is contained in his address to the Hindu community contained in the *Sambad Kaumadi* pointing out the need for their children to be instructed in the grammar of their own languages and to this end he published a Bengali grammar of his own (*Gauḍīya Vyākaraḍ*) in 1833. His earliest Persian work, however, entitled *Tuhfatul-ul-Muwahhiddin* (Gift to Deists), 1803 – 4, was never translated into Bengali. It claims belief in a creator, the existence of the soul and life after death, to be the basic tenets of all religions and dismisses other beliefs such as belief in miracles, anthropomorphic deities, and salvation through the correct performance of rites as irrational.

The emphasis on logic and reason characteristic of this early radical treatise reappears in his later writings and activities dominating his whole approach to religion. It is to be found in his defence of Hinduism against the attacks of Christian missionaries. While he acknowledged Hindu image worship to be irrational and contrary to Upanishadic teaching, the Christian doctrines of the Trinity, transubstantiation and atonement through Christ were equally illogical and contrary to the precepts of Jesus. Christianity was as much at the mercy of prejudice and superstition as Hinduism in this respect and nothing could be gained from denunciations based on mutual misrepresentation.

His emphasis on rationality is to be found also in the formation of the Brāhmo Samāj, a society founded by him in 1828 to promote a lofty theism and the restoration of religious purity within Hinduism with no image or likeness of the Eternal, Immutable Being who is the author and preserver of the universe. He accomplishes his aim through the worship of the one God of all religions with readings from the Vedas and the Upanishads, hymn singing and expository sermons. Though lacking in popular appeal because of its intellectual bent, the Brāhmo Samāj did succeed in creating an atmosphere of liberalism and rationality and in providing a meeting place for people of similar religious views and a forum for the reinterpretation of the Hindu tradition.

Described as the greatest creative personality of the nineteenth century, Roy sought above all to build a bridge between the old and new worlds through mutual respect and understanding. The spirituality of the East, he believed, ought to be harmonized with Western science and technology for the benefit of mankind. His contribution in the pursuit of this goal was such that it could not be ignored by the reformers who came after him and in that respect he fully deserves his place of eminence in the history of India.

RĀMMOHUN ROY

Idolatry and the Defence of Hindu Theism

From a translation of an abridgement of the Vedānta, a work of Brahmanic theology, establishing the unity of the Supreme Being and entitled 'To the Believers of the only true God.'

The greater part of Brahmans, as well as of other sects of Hindoos, are quite incapable of justifying that idolatry which they continue to practise. When questioned on the subject, in place of adducing reasonable arguments in support of their conduct, they conceive it fully sufficient to quote their ancestors as positive authorities! And some of them are become very ill-disposed towards me, because I have forsaken idolatry for the worship of the true and eternal God! In order therefore, to vindicate my own faith and that of our early forefathers, I have been endeavouring, for some time past, to convince my countrymen of the true meaning of our sacred books; and to prove, that my aberration deserves not the opprobrium which some unreflecting persons have been so ready to throw upon me . . .

In pursuance of my vindication, I have to the best of my abilities translated this hitherto unknown work, as well as an abridgement thereof, into the Hindoostanee and Bengalee languages, and distributed them, free of cost, among my own countrymen, as widely as circumstances have possibly allowed. The present is an endeavour to render an abridgment of the same into English, by which I expect to prove to my European friends, that the superstitious practices which deform the Hindoo religion have nothing to do with the pure spirit of its dictates!

I have observed that, both in their writings and conversation, many Europeans feel a wish to palliate and soften the features of Hindoo idolatry; and are inclined to inculcate, that all objects of worship are considered by their votaries as emblematical representations of the Supreme Divinity! If this were indeed the case, I might perhaps be led into some examination of the subject: but the truth is, the Hindoos of the present day have no such views of the subject, but firmly believe in the real existence of innumerable gods and goddesses, who possess, in their own departments, full and independent power; and to propitiate them, and not the true God, are temples erected and ceremonies performed. There can be no doubt, however, and it is my whole design to prove, that every rite has its derivation from the allegorical adoration of the true Deity; but at the present day all this is forgotten, and among many it is even heresy to mention it! . . .

My constant reflections on the inconvenient, or rather injurious rites introduced by the peculiar practice of Hindoo idolatry which more than any other pagan worship, destroys the texture of society, together with compassion for my countrymen, have compelled me to use every possible effort to awaken them from their dream of error: and by making them acquainted with their scriptures, enable them to contemplate with true devotion the unity and omnipresence of Nature's God.[1]

A defence of Hindu theism in reply to Śankara Śastri, head English master at the Madras Government College, attacking Rāmmohun Roy's views and advocating the worship of divine attributes as deities.

The learned gentleman says that 'Their (the attributes and incarnations) worship under various representations, by means of consecrated objects, is prescribed by the scripture to the human race, by way of mental exercises,' etc. I cannot admit that the worship of these attributes under various representations, by means of consecrated objects, has been prescribed by the Veda to the HUMAN RACE; as this kind of worship of consecrated objects is enjoined by the Sastra to those only who are incapable of raising their minds to the notion of an invisible Supreme Being. I have quoted several authorities for this assertion in my Preface to the Isopanishad, and beg to repeat here one or two of them: 'The vulgar look for their God in water; men of more extended knowledge in celestial bodies; the ignorant in wood, bricks, and stones; but learned men in the Universal Soul.' 'Thus corresponding to the nature of different powers or qualities, numerous figures have been invented for the benefit of those who are not possessed of sufficient understanding.' Permit me in this instance to ask, whether every Mussulman in Turkey and Arabia, from the highest to the lowest, every Protestant Christian at least of Europe, and many followers of Kabir and Nanak, do worship God without the assistance of consecrated objects? If so, how can we suppose that the human race is not capable of adoring the Supreme Being without the puerile practice of having recourse to visible objects?

. . . The learned gentleman is of opinion that the attributes of God exist distinctly from God and he compares the relation between God and these attributes to that of a king to his ministers, as he says: 'If a person be desirous to visit an earthly prince, he ought to be introduced in the first instance by his ministers', etc; and 'in like manner the grace of God ought to be obtained by the grace through the worship of his attributes.' This opinion, I am extremely sorry to find, is directly contrary to all the Vedanta doctrines interpreted to us by the most revered Sankaracharya, which are real adwaita or non-duality; they affirm that God has no second that may be possessed of eternal existence, either of the same nature with himself or of a different nature from him, nor any second of that nature that might be called either his part or his quality . . .

The Veda very often calls the Supreme Existence by the epithets of Existence, Wise, and Eternal and assigns as the reason for adopting such epithets, that the Veda in the first instance speaks of God according to the human idea, which views quality separately from person, in order to facilitate our comprehension of objects. In case these attributes should be supposed, as the learned gentleman asserts, to be separate existences, it necessarily follows, that they must be either eternal or non-eternal. The former case, viz, the existence of a plurality of beings imbued like God himself with the property of eternal duration, strikes immediately at the root of all the doctrines relative to the unity of the Supreme Being contained in the Vedanta. By the latter sentiment, namely, that the power and attributes of God are not eternal, we are led at once, into the belief that the nature of God is susceptible of change, and consequently that He is not eternal, which makes no inconsiderable step towards atheism itself. These are the obvious and dangerous consequences, resulting from the learned gentleman's doctrine, that the attributes of the Supreme Being are distinct existences.[2]

A second defence of Hindu theism and the monotheistic system of the Vedas in reply to the attack of an advocate for idolatry reputed to be the work of a learned Brahmin from Calcutta.

As to the custom or practice to which the learned Braham so often refers in defence of idolatry, I have already, I presume, explained in the Preface of the *Isopanishad*, the accidental circumstances which have caused idol-worship to flourish throughout the greater part of India; but, as the learned Brahman has not condescended to notice any of my remarks on this subject, I beg leave to repeat here a part of them.

'Many learned Brahmans are perfectly aware of the absurdity
of idolatry, and are well informed of the nature of the pure mode
of divine worship; but as in the rites, ceremonies, and festivals of
idolatry, they find the source of their comforts and fortune, they
not only never fail to protect idol-worship from all attacks, but
even advance and encourage it to the utmost of their power, by
keeping the knowledge of their scriptures concealed from the rest
of the people.' And again: 'It is, however, evident to every one
possessed of common sense, that custom or fashion is quite different from divine faith; the latter proceeding from spiritual
authorities and correct reasoning, and the former being merely
the fruit of vulgar caprice. What can justify a man, who believes
in the inspiration of his religious books, in neglecting the direct
authorities of the same works, and subjecting himself entirely to
custom and fashion, which are liable to perpetual changes, and
depend upon popular whim? But it cannot be passed unnoticed,
that those who practise idolatry, and defend it under the shield of
custom, have been violating their customs almost every twenty
years, for the sake of a little convenience, or to promote their
worldly advantages.' . . .

The learned Brahman attempts to prove the impossibility of an
adoration of the Deity, saying . . . 'That which cannot be considered, cannot be worshipped.' Should the learned Brahman
consider a full conception of the nature, essence, or qualities of
the Supreme Being, or a physical picture truly representing the
Almighty power, with offerings of flowers, leaves, and viands, as
essential to adoration, I agree with the learned Brahman with
respect to the impossibility of the worship of God. But, should
adoration imply only the elevation of the mind to the conviction
of the existence of the Omnipresent Deity, as testified by His wise
and wonderful works, and continual contemplation of His power
as so displayed, together with a constant sense of the gratitude
which we naturally owe Him, for our existence, sensation, and
comfort — I never will hesitate to assert, that His adoration is not
only possible, and practicable, but even incumbent upon every
rational creature.[3]

Christianity and Hinduism

*The superiority of Christianty and the precepts of Christ compared
with the idolatrous nature of Hinduism and its caste distinctions is
the topic of the following extracts from the letters of Rāmmohun
Roy.*

Rāmmohun Roy to Mr John Digby, England, 1816 – 7

I take this opportunity of giving you a summary account of my proceedings since the period of your departure from India.

The consequence of my long and uninterrupted researches into religious truth has been that I have found the doctrines of Christ more conducive to moral principles, and better adapted for the use of rational beings, than any others which have come to my knowledge; and have also found Hindus in general more superstitious and miserable, both in performance of their religious rites, and in their domestic concerns, than the rest of the known nations of the earth. I, therefore, with a view of making them happy and comfortable both here and hereafter, not only employed verbal arguments against the absurdities of the idolatry practised by them, but also translated their most revered theological work, namely, Vedant, into Bengali and Hindustani and also several chapters of the Ved, in order to convince them that the Unity of God, and absurdity of idolatry are evidently pointed out by their own scriptures. I, however, in the beginning of my pursuits met with the greatest opposition from their self-interested leaders, the Brahmins, and was deserted by my nearest relations; I consequently felt extremely melancholy; in that critical situation, the only comfort that I had was the consoling and rational conversation of my European friends; especially those of Scotland and England.

I now, with the greatest pleasure, inform you that several of my countrymen have risen superior to their prejudices; many are inclined to seek for the truth, and a great number of those who dissented from me have now coincided with me in opinion.

Extract from a letter dated 18 January 1828

I agree with you that in point of vices the Hindus are not worse than the generality of Christians in Europe and America; but I regret to say that the present system of religion adhered to by the Hindus is not well calculated to promote their political interest. The distinction of castes, introducing innumerable divisions and sub-divisions among them, has entirely deprived them of patriotic feeling, and the multitude of religious rites and ceremonies and the laws of purification have totally disqualified them from undertaking any difficult enterprise . . . It is, I think necessary that some changes should take place in their religion, at least for the sake of their political advantage and social comfort. I fully agree with you that there is nothing so sublime as the precepts taught by Christ, and that there is nothing equal to the simple doctrine he inculcated.[4]

Conversion

From a letter addressed to the Reverend Henry Ware of Cambridge (U.S.A.) 2 February 1824, on the prospects of Christianity and the means of promoting its reception in India.

I have now prepared such replies to those questions as my knowledge authorises and my conscience permits; and now submit them to your judgment. There is one question at the concluding part of your letter, (to wit, 'Whether it be desirable that the inhabitants of India should be converted to Christianity, in what degree desirable, and for what reasons?') which I pause to answer, as I am led to believe, from reason, what is set forth in the scripture, that 'in every nation he that feareth God and worketh righteousness is accepted with him,' in whatever form of worship he may have been taught to glorify God. Nevertheless, I presume to think, that Christianity, if properly inculcated, has a greater tendency to improve the moral, and political state of mankind, than any other known religious system.

It is impossible for me to describe the happiness I feel at the idea that so great a body of free, enlightened, and powerful people, like your countrymen, have engaged in purifying the religion of Christ from those absurd, idolatorous doctrines and practices, with which the Greek, Roman, and Barbarian converts to Christianity have mingled it from time to time.[5]

Extract from a letter addressed by Raja Rāmmohun Roy to a gentleman of Baltimore, dated Calcutta, 27 October 1822.

I have now every reason to hope, that the truths of Christianity will not be much longer kept hidden under the veil of heathen doctrines and practices, gradually introduced among the followers of Christ since many lovers of truth are zealously engaged in rendering the religion of Jesus clear from corruption.

I admire the zeal of the Missionaries sent to this country, but disapprove of the means they have adopted. In the performance of their duty, they always begin with such obscure doctrines as are calculated to excite ridicule instead of respect, towards the religion which they wish to promulgate. The accompanying pamphlets, called 'The Brahmunical Magazine,' and published by a Brahmun, are a proof of my assertion. The last number of this publication has remained unanswered for twelve months.

If a body of men attempt to upset a system of doctrines generally established in a country, and to introduce another system, they are, in my humble opinion, in duty bound to prove the truth, or, at least, the superiority of their own.

It is, however, a great satisfaction to my conscience to find, that the doctrines inculcated by Jesus and his apostles, are quite different from those human inventions, which the Missionaries are persuaded to profess, and entirely consistent with reason, and the revelation delivered by Moses and the prophets. I am, therefore, anxious to support them, even at the risk of my own life. I rely much on the force of truth, which will, I am sure, ultimately prevail. Our number is comparatively small, but I am glad to inform you, that none of them can be justly charged with the want of zeal and prudence.

I wish to add, in order that you may set me right, if you find me mistaken, — my view of Christianity is, that in representing all mankind as the children of one eternal father, it enjoins them to love one another, without making any distinction of country, caste, colour, or creed; notwithstanding they may be justified in the sight of the Creator in manifesting their respect towards each other, according to the property of their actions, and the reasonableness of their religious opinions and observance.[6]

The Precepts of Jesus

From the introduction to 'The Precepts of Jesus', (Calcutta, 1820), compiled by Rāmmohun Roy with translations into Sanskrit and Bengali.

Voluminous works, written by learned men of particular sects for the purpose of establishing the truth, consistency, rationality, and priority of their own peculiar doctrines, contain such variety of arguments, that I cannot hope to be able to adduce here any new reasonings of sufficient novelty and force to attract the notice of my readers. Besides, in matters of religion particularly men in general, through prejudice and partiality to the opinions which they once form, pay little or no attention to opposite sentiments (however reasonable they may be) and often turn a deaf ear to what is most consistent with the laws of nature, and conformable to the dictates of human reason and divine revelation. At the same time, to those who are not biased by prejudice, and who are, by the grace of God, open to conviction, a simple enumeration and statement of the respective tenets of different sects may be a sufficient guide to direct their inquiries in ascertaining which of them is most consistent with the sacred traditions, and most acceptable to common sense. For these reasons, I decline entering into any discussion on those points, and confine my attention at present to the task of laying before my fellow-creatures the words of Christ, with a translation from the English into Sanscrit, and the language of Bengal. I feel persuaded that by separating from the other matters contained in the New Testament, the moral precepts found in that book, these will be more likely to produce the desirable effect of improving the hearts and minds of men of different persuasions and degrees of understanding.[7]

An appeal to the Christian public in defence of 'The Precepts of Jesus' by a Friend of the Truth (1820). *Rāmmohun Roy defends his work under this pseudonym against disapproving critics.*

The editor of the 'Friend of India', and the respective Reviewer, both not only disapprove absolutely the plan adopted by the Compiler in separating the moral doctrines of the Books of the New Testament ascribed to the four Evangelists from the mysteries and historical matters therein contained, but even blame him as an injurer of the cause of truth.

The Reviewer charges the compiler with inconsistency, (p.27) because he has termed the Precepts collected by him, a code of Religion and Morality, while, as the Reviewer supposes, they form only a code of morality and not of religion. It is already explained in paragraph 2nd that the Compiler has introduced those Precepts of Jesus under the denomination of the moral sayings of the New Testament, taking the word moral in its wide sense, as including our conduct to God, to each other and to ourselves; and to avoid the least possibility of misunderstanding the term, he has carefully particularised the sense in which he accepted that word by the latter sentence, 'This simple code of Religion and Morality, (meaning by the former, those precepts which treat of our duty to God, and by the latter, such as relate to our duties to mankind, and to ourselves), is so admirably calculated to elevate men's ideas to high and liberal notions of one God, &c.,' . . . 'and is also so well fitted to regulate the conduct of the human race in the discharge of their various duties to God, to themselves, and to society, &c.' In conformity to the design thus expressed, he has collected all the sayings that have a tendency to those ends. The Compiler, however, observes with regret, that neither this language nor this fact, has afforded to the Reviewer satisfactory evidence of his intention nor sufficed to save him from the unexpected imputation of inconsistency.[8]

A second appeal to the Christian public by Rāmmohun Roy in defence of 'The Precepts of Jesus'.

The contents of the following Treatise are included under these two propositions:— 1st, That the Precepts of Jesus, which teach that love to God is manifested in beneficence towards our fellow-creatures, are a sufficient Guide to Peace and Happiness; and 2ndly, That the omnipresent God, who is the only proper object of religious veneration, is one and undivided in person . . .

The Reverend Editor labours in his Review to establish two points — the truth and excellency of the miraculous relations and of the dogmas found in the scriptural writings; and, 2ndly, the insufficiency of the compiled Precepts of Jesus alone to lead to salvation, unless accompanied with the important doctrines of the Godhead of Jesus and his atonement.

As the Compiler neither in his Introduction to the Precepts of Jesus, nor in his defence of those Precepts, has expressed the least doubt as to the truth of any part of the Gospels, the arguments adduced by the learned Editor to demonstrate the truth and excellence of the authority on which they rest, are, I am inclined to think, quite superfluous, and foreign to the matter in question.

The only reason assigned by the Compiler, (in the Introduction), for separating the Precepts from the abstruse doctrines and miraculous relations of the New Testament, are, that the former 'are liable to the doubts and disputes of Freethinkers and Anti-christians, and the latter are capable at best of carrying little weight with the natives of this part of the globe, the fabricated tales handed down to them being of a more wonderful nature.'[9]

Defence of Hinduism

Objections to Hinduism were contained in a Bengali Weekly newspaper called 'Samachar Darpan' produced by Christian missionaries at Serampore on 14 July 1821. Doubts were expressed concerning Vedāntic teaching about māyā; the teaching of the Nyāya Sāstra about God and creation; the dualism of the Sāṁkhya system; and the interpretation of sacrificial rites in the Mīmāṁsā Sāstra. Rāmmohun Roy's reply was denied publication in the 'Samachar Darpan' and hence published in his own 'Brahmunical Magazine' prefaced with an explanation of the origin of the controversy of which the following is an extract:

It is well-known to the whole world, that no people on earth are more tolerant than the Hindoos, who believe all men to be equally within the reach of Divine beneficence, which embraces the good of every religious sect and denomination; therefore it cannot be imagined that my object in publishing this Magazine was to oppose Christianity; but I was influenced by the conviction that persons who travel to a distant country for the purpose of overturning the opinions of its inhabitants and introducing their own, ought to be prepared to demonstrate that the latter are more reasonable than the former.

Extracts from Roy's reply to the missionary objections

You, in the first place, attempt to shew the folly of the Vedanta, and for that purpose recount its doctrines, saying 'that it teaches God to be one, eternal, unlimited by past, present or future time, without form or desires, beyond the apprehension of the senses, pure intellect, omnipresent, without defect and perfect in every respect; and that there is no other real existence except him, nor is the soul different from him; that this visible world is created by his power, i.e., Maya, and that Maya is opposed to a true knowledge of God (i.e., after the acquisition of a knowledge of God the effect of Maya, which is the universe, no longer continues to appear as a real existence, in the same manner as when a piece of rope is mistaken for a snake the misconceived existence of the snake is destroyed by a knowledge of the real existence of the rope, or as the palace of Gandharvas seen in a dream ceases to appear immediately after the expiration of the dream).' Now, you allege these faults in these doctrines. Ist. An admission of their

truth either brings reproach upon God or establishes the
supremacy and eternity both of God and of Maya. As you have
not stated what reproach attaches to God from the admission of
these doctrines, I am unable to answer the first alternative. If you
kindly particularize it, I may endeavour to make a reply. As to the
latter alternative respecting the supremacy and eternity of Maya, I
beg to answer, that the followers to the Vedanta (in common with
the Christians and Mussulmans who believe God to be eternal)
profess also the eternity of all his attributes. Maya is the creating
power of the eternal God, and consequently it is declared by the
Vedanta to be eternal. 'Maya has no separate existence; it is the
power of God and is known by its effects as heat is the power of
fire and has no separate existence, yet is known from its effects'
(quoted in the Vedanta). Should it be improper to declare the
attributes of God eternal, then such impropriety applies univer-
sally to all religious systems, and the Vedanta cannot be alone
accused of this impropriety.

In like manner, in the Vedanta and in other systems, as well as
in common experience, the superiority of substance over its
qualities is acknowledged. The Vedanta has never stated, in any
instance, the supremacy both of God and of Maya, that you
should charge the Vedanta with absurdity.

The second fault which you find, is that if the soul be the same
as God, nothing can justify the belief that the soul is liable to be
rewarded and punished according to its good and evil works; for
such a belief would amount to the blasphemy that God also is
liable to reward and punishment.

I reply — The world, as the Vedanta says, is the effect of Maya,
and is material; but God is mere spirit, whose particular influences being shed upon certain material objects are called souls in
the same manner as the reflections of the sun are seen on water
placed in various vessels. As these reflections of the sun seem to
be moved by the motion of the water of those vessels without
effecting any motion in the sun, so souls, being, as it were, the
reflections of the Supreme Spirit on matter, seem to be affected
by the circumstances that influence matter, without God being
affected by such circumstances. As some reflections are bright
from the purity of the water on which they are cast, while others
seem obscure owing to its foulness, so some souls are more pure
from the purity of the matter with which they are connected,
while others are dull owing to the dullness of matter.

As the reflections of the sun, though without light proper to
themselves, appear splendid from their connection with the

illuminating sun, so the soul, though not true intellect, seems intellectual and acts as if it were real spirit from its actual relation to the Universal Intellect: and as from the particular relations of the sun to the water placed in different pots, various reflections appear resembling the same sun in nature and differing from it in qualities; and again as these cease to appear on the removal of the water, so through the peculiar relation of various material objects to one Supreme Spirit numerous souls appear and seem as performing good and evil works, and also receiving their consequences; and as soon as that relation ceases, they, at that very minute cease to appear distinctly from their original. Hence God is one, and the soul, although it is not in fact of a different origin from God, is yet liable to experience the consequences of good and evil works; but this liability of the soul to reward or punishment cannot render God liable to either.

The third fault alleged by you, is, that from the doctrines alluded to, the perfection of God and his sufficiency cannot be maintained. This is your position, but you have advanced no arguments to prove it. If you afterwards do, I may consider the force of them. If you, however, mean by the position that if souls be considered as parts of God, as declared by the Vedanta, and proceeding from the Supreme Spirit, God must be insufficient and imperfect; I will in this case refer you to the above answer, that is, although the reflections of the sun owe to him their existence and depend upon and return to the same sun, yet this circumstance does not tend to prove the insufficiency or imperfection of the sun . . .[10]

Unitarianism

From a speech delivered at a meeting of the Unitarian Association, London, held in his honour in which he refers to his pride at being called a fellow-labourer and being admitted to the Society as a brother.

I am not sensible that I have done anything to deserve being called a promoter of this cause; but with respect to your faith I may observe, that I too believe in the one God, and that I believe in almost all the doctrines that you do: but I do this for my own salvation and for my own peace. For the objects of your Society I must confess that I have done very little to entitle me to your gratitude or such admiration of my conduct. What have I done? — I do not know what I have done! — If I have ever rendered

any services they must be very trifling — very trifling I am sure. I
laboured under many disadvantages. In the first instance, the
Hindoos and the Brahmins, to whom I am related, are all hostile
to the cause; and even many Christians there are more hostile to
our common cause than the Hindoos and the Brahmins. I have
honour for the appellation of Christians; but they always tried to
throw difficulties and obstacles in the way of the principles of
Unitarian Christianity. I have found some of these here; but more
there. They abhor the notion of simple precepts. They always lay
a stress on mystery and mystical points, which serve to delude
their followers; and the consequence is, that we meet with such
opposition in India that our progress is very slight; and I feel
ashamed on my side that I have not made any progress that might
have placed me on a footing with my fellow-labourers in this part
of the globe. However, if this is the true system of Christianity, it
will prevail, notwithstanding all the opposition that may be made
to it. Scripture seconds your system of religion, common sense is
also on your side; while power and prejudice are on the side of
your opponents. There is a battle going on between reasons, scripture and common sense; and wealth, power and prejudice. These
three have been struggling with the other three; but I am convinced that your success, sooner or later, is certain. I feel over-
exhausted, and therefore conclude with an expression of my
heartfelt thanks for the honour that from time to time you have
conferred on me, and which I shall never forget to the last
moment of my existence.[11]

Suttee

*Report of a second conference between an advocate for and an oppo-
nent of the practice of burning widows alive, Calcutta, 1820*

Advocate. I allude . . . to the real reason for our anxiety to persuade widows to follow their husbands, and for our endeavours to
burn them pressed down with ropes: *viz.*, that women are by
nature of inferior understanding, without resolution, unworthy of
trust, subject to passions, and void of virtuous knowledge; they,
according to the precepts of the Sastra, are not allowed to marry
again after the demise of their husbands, and consequently
despair at once of all worldly pleasure; hence it is evident, that
death to these unfortunate widows is preferable to existence; for

the great difficulty which a widow may experience by living a purely ascetic life, as prescribed by the Sastras, is obvious; therefore, if she do not perform Concremation, it is probable that she may be guilty of such acts as may bring disgrace upon her paternal and maternal relations, and those that may be connected with her husband. Under these circumstances, we instruct them from their early life in the idea of Concremation, holding out to them heavenly enjoyments in company with their husbands, as well as the beatitude of their relations, both by birth and marriage, and their reputation in this world. From this many of them, on the death of their husbands, become desirous of accompanying them; but to remove every chance of their trying to escape from the blazing fire, in burning them we first tie them down to the pile.

Opponent. The reason you have now assigned for burning widows alive is indeed your true motive, as we are well aware; but the faults which you have imputed to women are not planted in their constitution by nature; it would be, therefore, grossly criminal to condemn that sex to death merely from precaution. By ascribing to them all sorts of improper conduct, you have indeed successfully persuaded the Hindu community to look down upon them as contemptible and mischievous creatures, whence they have been subjected to constant miseries. I have, therefore, to offer a few remarks on this head.

Women are in general inferior to men in bodily strength and energy; consequently the male part of the community, taking advantage of their corporeal weakness, have denied to them those excellent merits that they are entitled to by nature, and afterwards they are apt to say that women are naturally incapable of acquiring those merits. But if we give the subject consideration, we may easily ascertain whether or not our accusation against them is consistent with justice. As to their inferiority in point of understanding, when did you ever afford them a fair opportunity of exhibiting their natural capacity? How then can you accuse them of want of understanding? If, after instruction in knowledge and wisdom, a person cannot comprehend or retain what has been taught him, we may consider him as deficient; but as you keep women generally void of education and acquirements, you cannot, therefore, in justice pronounce on their inferiority . . .

Secondly. You charge them with want of resolution, at which I feel exceedingly surprised: for we constantly perceive, in a country where the name of death makes the male shudder, that the female, from her firmness of mind, offers to burn with the corpse of her deceased husband; and yet you accuse those women of deficiency in point of resolution.

Thirdly. With regard to their trustworthiness, let us look minutely into the conduct of both sexes, and we may be enabled to ascertain which of them is the most frequently guilty of betraying friends. If we enumerate such women in each village or town as have been deceived by men, and such men as have been betrayed by women, I presume that the number of the deceived women would be found ten times greater than that of the betrayed men . . .

In the fourth place, with respect to their subjection to the passions, this may be judged of by the custom of marriage as to the respective sexes; for one man may marry two or three, sometimes even ten wives and upwards; while a women, who marries but one husband, desires at his death to follow him, forsaking all worldly enjoyments, or to remain leading the austere life of an ascetic.

Fifthly. The accusation of the want of virtuous knowledge is an injustice. Observe what pain, what slighting, what contempt, and what afflictions their virtue enables them to support! How many Kulin[12] Brahmans are there who marry ten or fifteen wives for the sake of money, that never see the greater number of them after the day of marriage, and visit others only three or four times in the course of their life. Still amongst those women, most, even without seeing or receiving any support from their husbands, living dependent on their fathers or brothers, and suffering much distress, continue to preserve their virtue; and when Brahmans, or those of other tribes, bring their wives to live with them, what misery do the women not suffer? At marriage the wife is recognized as half of her husband, but in after-conduct they are treated worse than inferior animals . . . What I lament is, that, seeing the women thus dependent and exposed to every misery, you feel for them no compassion, that might exempt them from being tied down and burnt to death.[13]

An anti-suttee petition presented to the House of Commons in opposition to an appeal of the advocates of suttee to re-establish the rite.

The humble Petition of the undersigned Natives of India.
   Sheweth,

That a practice has prevailed throughout India, particularly in Bengal, of burning those widows on the funeral piles of their deceased husbands, who could be induced to offer themselves as voluntary sacrifices.

That this barbarous and inhuman practice has been happily abolished by the Government of the Right Honourable Lord William Cavendish Bentinck, who has thus conferred an inestimable benefit on the native population of India.

That the regulation prohibiting the practice has been received with gratitude by many, while the majority of the native population have remained passive and acquiescent, although nearly a twelvemonth has elapsed since the abolition took place . . .

That your petitioners have, however, learned that a number of natives, professing to be attached to the ancient practice, have prepared a petition to your Honourable House, soliciting the re-establishment of the rite of burning their widows; and therefore to prevent your Honourable House from supposing that their sentiments are those of the whole native population, your petitioners respectivelly present themselves to the notice of your Honourable House, and pray that the Regulation of the local government may be confirmed and enforced.

That your petitioners cannot permit themselves to suppose that such a practice, abhorrent to all the feelings of nature, the obligations of society, and the principles of good government, will receive the sanction of your Honourable House, much less that, having been abolished, the British name and character will be dishonoured by its re-establishment.

That your petitioners confidently rely on receiving from your Honourable House a full and final confirmation of the Act of the Governor-General in Council abolishing the rite of widow-burning.[14]

From a letter to James Munro MacNabb, 6 March 1820, requesting him to lay before Lady Hastings, Countess of Loudon, Roy's thoughts on suttee.

Her Ladyship's universal character for every humane and Christianlike virtue makes me confident that she cannot view with indifference the miserable and violent death to which the unfortunate females of India, and more particularly of Bengal in recent years . . . are subjected . . . I (hope) that the glory of saving

thousands of unhappy women from cruel murder will not be left
to any future ruler of these provinces . . . Except among some few
tribes and families these murders are not favoured.[15]

Education

From a letter to the Right Honourable William Pitt, Lord Amherst.

My Lord,
   Humbly reluctant as the natives of India are to obtrude upon
the notice of Government the sentiments they entertain on any
public measure, there are circumstances when silence would be
carrying this respectful feeling to culpable excess. The present
Rulers of India, coming from a distance of many thousand miles
to govern a people whose language, literature, manners, customs,
and ideas are almost entirely new and strange to them, cannot
easily become so intimately acquainted with their real circumstances, as the natives of the country are themselves. We would
therefore be guilty of a gross dereliction of duty to ourselves, and
afford our Rulers just ground of complaint at our apathy, did we
omit on occasions of importance like the present to supply them
with such accurate information as might enable them to devise
and adopt measures calculated to be beneficial to the country, and
thus second by our local knowledge and experience their declared
benevolent intentions for its improvement.
   The establishment of a new Sangscrit School in Calcutta evinces
the laudable desire of the Government to improve the natives of
India by Education, a blessing for which they must ever be
grateful; and every well wisher of the human race must be
desirous that the efforts made to promote it should be guided by
the most enlightened principles, so that the stream of intelligence
may flow into the most useful channels.
   When this Seminary of learning was proposed, we understood
that the Government in England had ordered a considerable sum
of money to be annually devoted to the instruction of its Indian
Subjects. We were filled with sanguine hopes that this sum would
be laid out in employing European Gentlemen of talents and
education to instruct the natives of India in Mathematics, Natural
Philosophy, Chemistry, Anatomy and other useful Sciences,
which the Nations of Europe have carried to a degree of

perfection that has raised them above the inhabitants of other parts of the world.

While we looked forward with pleasing hope to the dawn of knowledge thus promised to the rising generation, our hearts were filled with mingled feeling of delight and gratitude; we already offered up thanks to Providence for inspiring the most generous and enlightened of the Nations of the West with the glorious ambitions of planting in Asia the Arts and Sciences of modern Europe.

We now find that the Government are establishing a Sangscrit school under Hindoo Pundits to impart such knowledge as is already current in India. This seminary (similar in character to those which existed in Europe before the time of Lord Bacon) can only be expected to load the minds of youth with grammatical niceties and metaphysical distinctions of little or no practicable use to the possessors or to society. The pupils will there acquire what was known two thousand years ago, with the addition of vain and empty subtleties since produced by speculative men, such as is already commonly taught in all parts of India.

The Sangscrit language, so difficult that almost a life time is necessary for its perfect acquisition, is well known to have been for ages a lamentable check on the diffusion of knowledge; and the learning concealed under this almost impervious veil is far from sufficient to reward the labour of acquiring it. But if it were thought necessary to perpetuate this language for the sake of the portion of the valuable information it contains, this might be much more easily accomplished by other means than the establishment of a new Sangscrit College; for there have been always and are now numerous professors of Sangscrit in the different parts of the country engaged in teaching this language as well as the other branches of literature, which are to be the object of the new Seminary. Therefore their more diligent cultivation, if desirable, would be effectually promoted by holding out premiums and granting certain allowances to those most eminent Professors, who have already undertaken on their own account to teach them and would by such rewards be stimulated to still greater exertions.

From these considerations, as the sum set apart for the instruction of the Natives of India was intended by the Government in England, for the improvement of its Indian subjects, I beg leave to state, with due deference to your Lordship's exalted situation, that if the plans now adopted be followed, it will completely defeat the object proposed; since no improvement can be expected from inducing young men to consume a dozen of years of the most valuable period of their lives in acquiring the niceties of the Byakurun or Sangscrit Grammar . . .

But as the improvement of the native population is the object of the Government, it will consequently promote a more liberal and enlightened system of instruction, embracing mathematics, natural philosophy, chemistry and anatomy with other useful sciences which may be accomplished with the sum proposed by employing a few gentlemen of talent and learning educated in Europe, and providing a college furnished with the necessary books, instruments and other apparatus.

In representing this subject to your Lordship I conceive myself discharging a solemn duty which I owe to my countrymen and also to that enlightened Sovereign and Legislature which have extended their benevolent cares to this distant land actuated by a desire to improve its inhabitants and I therefore humbly trust you will excuse the liberty I have taken in thus expressing my sentiments to your Lordship.

CALCUTTA,   I have etc.
The 11th December 1823   Rammohun Roy.[16]

NOTES

1 *English Works of Raja Rammohun Roy*, edited by Dr Kalidas Nag and Debajyoti Burman, (Calcutta, 1945 – 51), Part II (1946), 59 – 61.
2 Ibid., 89 – 90.
3 Ibid., 106 – 16.
4 Ibid., Part IV (1947) 94 – 6.
5 Ibid., 43 – 4.
6 Ibid., 85 – 6.
7 Ibid., Part V (1948) 3 – 4.
8 Ibid., 59, 68 – 9.
9 Ibid., Part VI (1951) 1 – 2.
10 Ibid., Part II (1946) 140, 143 – 5, 147 – 50.
11 Ibid., Part IV (1947) 84.
12 Kulin: an élite group of Bengal Brahmins.
13 *English Works*, Part III (1947) 124 – 7.
14 Ibid., 137 – 8.
15 An extract from a letter in the MacNabb archives at Killin, Tayside, Scotland, supplied by John C.P. Riddy.
16 *English Works*, Part IV (1946), 105 – 8.

REFERENCES

English Works of Raja Rammohun Roy, Part I – VI. Edited by Kalidas Nag and Debajyoti Burman, Calcutta: Sadharan Brahma Samaj, 1945 – 51.

Sophia Dobson Collet, *The Life and Letters of Raja Rammohun Roy.* Calcutta: Sadharan Brahmo Samaj, 1900. Third edition, 1962.

2

DEVENDRANĀTH TAGORE (1817 – 1905)

Devendranāth, eldest son of Dwārkanāth Tagore, was born in Calcutta, May 1817, into a wealthy family. Educated at the Hindu College he showed a great interest in religious questions from an early age and founded the association known as the Tatwabodhini Sabha in 1839 for the purpose of gaining knowledge of God and disseminating information about the religious heritage of India. His first contact with the Brahmo Samāj nine years after the death of its founder made him realize that the aims of the Sabha could more easily be attained through amalgamation with the Samāj and this was duly effected in 1843. He instituted reforms in the Samāj including the removal of caste distinctions, idolatry and incarnational doctrines in accordance with the trust deed and rejected the doctrine of the infallibility of the Vedas. His main aim was to propagate knowledge of Brahma as taught in the Upanishads.

He attracted many able young men to the movement including Keshub Chunder Sen and showed great enthusiasm for the purification of the Hindu religion and for the education of children. In 1845 he joined the campaign against Christian conversions through education provided in Christian schools and to combat this practice sought to establish a school for Hindu children where they might receive education free of charge. At a meeting in Calcutta attended by almost a thousand people it was resolved to found such a school and it was called the Hind-hitārthi (the well-wisher of Hindus). While Tagore approved of the efforts of Christians for the welfare of his fellow countrymen he did not believe that they had much to offer that would help India to develop its own religious heritage.

His opposition to idolatry reflected the views of Rāmmohan Roy. He refused invitations to pujas where image-worship was involved and even abstained from attending the shraddha ceremony of his father. He saw no hope of propagating the worship of Brahma while ceremonial rites and ceremonies were sanctioned and cited the Vedic sages in support of his views. He believed that the ultimate good of India would derive from the rejection of Tantric and Puranic myths and legends and acceptance of the knowledge of Brahma as found in the Upanishads. It was the high regard that he had for the Upanishads that prompted his approval of Max Müller's translations which placed within the reach of European scholars the wisdom of the rishis which had previously been hidden from them in obscure manuscripts.

A man of sensitive spirit and deep religious feeling, Tagore in his later years inclined to mysticism. It was this sensitivity which made him embark on a journey to places of pilgrimage in the Himalayas to rekindle and nourish his spiritual life through communion with God and nature. His autobiography has many references to visions of the eternal God through contemplation of the starry heavens above and the divine spirit within. Dissensions which led ultimately to a split in the Samāj failed to disturb his equanimity or cause him to be despondent, and his love for his protégé Keshub Chunder Sen, though he could not accept his views, never wavered. It was his conviction that the fruit of man's work was in God's hand and that we should put our trust in him. It was this kind of piety that prompted Rāmakrishna to refer to him in complimentary terms and that earned him the title Maharshi — the great sage. He was not an ardent revolutionary or a dynamic reformer but his kindness and humility, his trust in God, his devotional spirit and his mystical inclinations together made him a significant personality among the reformers of Hinduism.

DEVENDRANĀTH TAGORE

Knowledge and Experience of God

His endeavour was to experience God not through blind faith as he calls it but by the light of knowledge.

Suddenly, as I thought and thought, a flash as of lightning broke through this darkness of despondency. I saw that knowledge of the material world is born of the senses and the objects of sight, sound, smell, touch, and taste. But together with this knowledge, I am also enabled to know that I am the knower. Simultaneously with the facts of seeing, touching, smelling, and thinking, I also come to know that it is I who see, touch, smell, and think. With the knowledge of objects comes the knowledge of the subject; with the knowledge of the body comes the knowledge of the spirit within. It was after a prolonged search for truth that I found this bit of light, as if a ray of sunshine had fallen on a place full of extreme darkness. I now realised that with the knowledge of the outer world we come to know our inner self. After this, the more I thought over it, the more did I recognise the sway of wisdom operating throughout the whole world. For us the sun and moon rise and set at regular intervals, for us the wind and rain are set in motion in the proper seasons. All these combine to fulfil the one design of preserving our life. Whose design is this? It cannot be the design of matter, it must be the design of mind. Therefore this universe is propelled by the power of an intelligent being. I saw that the child, as soon as born, drinks at its mother's breast. Who taught it to do this? He alone Who gave it life. Again, who put love into the mother's heart? Who but He that put milk into her breast. He is that God Who knows all our wants, Whose rule the universe obeys. When my mind's eye had opened thus far, the clouds of grief were in a great measure dispelled. I felt somewhat consoled.

One day, while thinking of these things, I suddenly recalled how, long ago, in my early youth, I had once realised the Infinite as manifested in the infinite heaven. Again I turned my gaze towards this infinite sky, studded with innumerable stars and planets, and saw the eternal God, and felt that this glory was His. He is Infinite Wisdom. He from Whom we have derived this limited knowledge of ours, and this body, its receptable, is Himself without form. He is without body or senses. He did not

shape this universe with His hands. By His will alone did He bring
it into existence. He is neither the Kali of Kalighat,[1] nor the family
Shaligram. Thus was the axe laid at the root of idolatry. In study-
ing the mechanism of creation, we find evidences of the wisdom
of the Creator. On looking at the starry sky, we feel that He is
infinite. By the help of this slender thread, His attributes became
clearer to my mind. I saw that no one could frustrate the will of
Him Who is Infinite Wisdom. Whatever He wills comes to pass.
We collect all the necessary materials, and then make a thing; He
by His will creates all the materials necessary for the making of
things. He is not only the maker of the world, but what is more,
He is its Creator. All created things are transient, corruptible,
changeable, and dependent. The Perfect wisdom that has created
them and is guiding them; that alone is eternal, incorruptible,
unchangeable, and self-dependent. That eternal, true and perfect
Being is the source of all good, and the object of all worship.[2]

Vision of Brahma

Then I went out and sat underneath an ashvattha tree and according to the teaching of the saints began meditating on the Spirit of
God dwelling within my soul. My mind was flooded with emotion, my eyes were filled with tears. All at once I saw the shining
vision of Brahma in the lotus core of my heart. A thrill passed
through my whole body, I felt a joy beyond all measure. But the
next moment I could see Him no more. On losing sight of that
beatific vision which destroys all sorrow, I suddenly rose from the
ground. A great sadness came over my spirit. Then I tried to see
Him again by force of contemplation, and found Him not. I
became as one stricken with disease, and would not be comforted.
Meanwhile I suddenly heard a voice in the air, 'In this life thou
shalt see Me no more. Those whose hearts have not been purified,
who have not attained the highest Yoga, cannot see Me. It was
only to stimulate thy love that I once appeared before thee.'[3]

Revelation of God in the Soul

Formerly when I used to see people worshipping factitious and
finite gods in their petty shrines I thought to myself, When shall I
see my own Infinite God face to face in the temple of this universe
and adore Him? This desire was then burning in my heart night

and day. Waking or asleep, this was my one wish, my only thought. Now, having seen in the heavens this radiant and immortal Being, all my desires were fulfilled, and all my torment was at an end.

I was satisfied with getting so much, but He was not content with giving so little. Hitherto He had existed beyond and outside myself; now He revealed Himself within me, I saw Him within my soul. The lord of the world-temple became the lord of my heart's shrine, and from thence I began to hear silent and solemn religious teachings. Fortune favoured me beyond all my expectations. I received more than I had ever hoped for, and scaled mountains, cripple though I was. I had not known how boundless was His mercy. The craving I had felt when seeking for Him increased a hundred-fold now that I had found Him . . .

Having found God, the current of my life flowed on swiftly, I gained fresh strength. The tide of my good fortune set in. I became a pilgrim on the path of love. I came to know now that He was the life of my life, the Friend of my heart; that I could not pass a single moment without Him.[4]

Light of the Soul

The sun does not shine there, nor the moon and the stars,
Nor do these lightnings, much less this fire.
When He shines, everything shines after Him:
By his light all this is lighted.

O Master, asked the disciple, how can I know God, the blissful, who has not been defined, whose infinite Majesty cannot be explained by words and is beyond our conception, and yet who is realised by those earnest seekers after truth who are devoted to Him? Who or what is there that can reveal Him? The guru answered, 'The sun, the moon and the stars cannot reveal God, nor these lightnings, much less this fire. In the bright presence of God the sun and the moon lose themselves, and they and every other lesser light become dark. It is only the light of the soul that can reveal the Lord. From the light of the soul you can have a faint idea of that Light of Truth.'

But what is this light of the soul? Look into your inner self, with the utmost attention of a mind abstracted from outward objects, and you will realise what the light of the soul is. When the sun is set, when the moon is not visible in the sky, when the fire is extinguished, what is the light that remains? It is only the light of the soul that is then visible. Realise this truth, even at this very moment . . .

How ignorant is he who seeks Him in the light that illumines the external world. In the external or material universe, we only behold the mere shadow of the Lord's wisdom and goodness; but within us is His light.[5]

Knowledge of God as Creator and Sustainer of the Universe

Deluded by ignorance, some thinkers say it is by the laws of nature — by the blind force of matter — that this wide world goes round; or others say that it is without any cause, by the force of Time alone. But I say — it is the glory of that Supreme Deity alone, by Whom this universal wheel is being turned:

> The whole world has come forth from the Living God. It exists by the power of the Living God.
> This Divine Being, Maker of the Universe, Supreme Soul, dwells for ever in the hearts of men.

These irrefutable truths concerning first principles have overflowed from the pure hearts of the Rishis . . .

The senses perceive only outward things, they cannot perceive that which is within. This is their shame:

> The self-existent God has made senses face outwards; hence they see outward things alone, not the soul within.
> Sometimes a wise man, desirous of immortality, closes his eyes and sees a Spirit dwelling in all things.

Hearing this precept, laying it to heart, and pondering deeply upon it, I saw God, not with fleshly eyes, but with the inner vision, from these Himalayan Hills, the holy land of Brahma. This was given me by the Upanishads. They say, 'All things are enveloped in God.' I enveloped all things with God. 'Now I have come to know that great sun-coloured Being beyond this darkness.'

> Henceforward I shall radiate light from my heart upon the world;
> For I have reached the Sun, and darkness has vanished.[6]

Doctrines of God, Soul and Creation

Again, when I saw in the Upanishads that the worship of Brahma leads to Nirvāna, my soul was dismayed at the idea:

Deeds, together with the sentient soul, all become one in Brahma.

If this means that the sentient soul loses its separate consciousness, then this is not the sign of salvation but a terrible extinction. What a vast difference between the eternal progress of the soul according to the Brāhma Dharma on the one hand, and this salvation by annihilation on the other! This Nirvāna-salvation of the Upanishads did not find a place in my heart.

Thus, in the year 1770 (A.D. 1848), the Brāhma Dharma was compiled in book form. The doctrines of Adwaitavada, Avatār vāda, and Māyāvāda[7] had no place therein. It was written in the Book of Brāhma Dharma that the relation of friendship subsisted between God and soul, and that they were constantly together: hence the doctrine of Monism was denied. The Brāhma Dharma says:

He Himself did not become anything.

He became not the material universe, neither trees nor creepers, neither birds, nor beasts, nor man. Hence the doctrine of Incarnation was denied. The Brāhma Dharma says:

He considered within Himself, and considering within Himself He created all that is.

This universe is the outcome of perfect truth. This universe is relative truth; its Creator is the Truth of Truth, the Absolute Truth. This universe is not dream-stuff, neither is it a mental illusion, but it exists in reality. The truth which has given it birth is the absolute truth, and this is relative truth. Thus the doctrine of Maya was denied.[8]

Brahmo-Samāj Reforms

After his first visit to the Samāj he took upon himself the task of reforming it. His reforms included: no caste distinctions, no incarnation restrictions and no idolatry.

The founder of the Samaj, the illustrius Rammohan Roy, had died nine years before in Bristol (England). I thought to myself that as the Brāhma-Samaj had been established for the worship of Brahma, our object would be the more easily attained by amalgamating the Tatwabodhini Sabha[9] with it.

When I first visited the Brāhma-Samaj, I noticed that the Vedas were recited in a private room from which Sudras were excluded. As the object of the Brāhma-Samaj was to popularise the worship of Brahma, and as it was expressly mentioned in the trust deed that all men should be able to worship Brahma without distinction of caste, I was deeply grieved to find the very reverse of this to be the practice. Again, I saw one day that Ramchandra Vidyāvagish's colleague, Ishwar Chandra Nyayaratna, was trying to establish, from the *vedi* of the Brāhma-Samaj, the fact of the incarnation of Ramchandra, King of Ayodhya. This struck me as being opposed to the spirit of Brāhma Dharma. In order to counteract this, I arranged that the Vedas should be read out in public, and forbade the exposition of the doctrine of incarnation from the *vedi*. In those days there was a dearth of learned men who could recite the Vedas and preach the doctrines of the Brāhma Dharma, so I set about finding pupils in order to train them up . . .

One day I was sitting in the printing office thinking on the want of the bond of a common religious feeling among members of the Brāhma-Samaj. People kept coming and going to and from the Samaj like the ebb and flow of the tide, but they were not bound together by any tie of religion. So when the number of visitors to the Samaj began to increase, I thought it necessary to pick and choose from among them. Some came really to worship, others came without any definite aim: whom should we recognise as the true worshipper of Brahma? Upon these considerations I decided that those who would take a vow to renounce idolatry and resolve to worship the one God, they alone would be regarded as Brāhmas. Considering that there was a Brāhma-Samaj, each member must of course be a Brāhma.[10]

Influence of Rāmmohan Roy and Views of Idolatry

I was the eldest son of my father. On any ceremonial occasion it was I who had to go from house to house inviting people. It was the time of the Durga Puja[11] in the month of Ashwin.[12] I went to invite Rammohan Roy to this festival, and said, 'Rammoni

Thakur[13] begs to invite you to attend the Puja for three days.'
Upon this he said, 'Brother, why come to me? Go and ask
Radhaprasad.' Now after all this lapse of time I understood the
purport and meaning of those words. Since then I inwardly
resolved that as Rammohan Roy did not take part in any image-
worship or idolatry, so would I not join in them either. I would
not worship any image, I would not bow down before any image,
I would not accept an invitation to any idolatrous worship. From
that time my mind was fully made up. I little knew then what a
fiery ordeal I was to pass through.

I formed a party with my brothers. We all resolved that we
would not go to the sanctuary during the Puja, and even if we
went none of us would bow down before the image. My father
used then to go to the sanctuary in the evening, at the time of the
arati, so that we too had to go there in deference to him. But when
the time came for saluting, and everybody bowed down to the
ground, we remained standing; nobody could see whether we performed the obeisance or not.

Whenever I came across idolatrous preachings in any *shastra* I
no longer felt any reverence for it. An erroneous impression was
then created in my mind that all our *shastras* were full of idolatry,
and that it was therefore impossible to extract from them truths
pertaining to the formless and changeless Deity.[14]

I did not know before that the god Agni held such supremacy
amongst us. From my childhood I had seen that nothing could be
done without the *Shaligram*. In marriage and other ceremonies, at
all pujas and religious festivals, you must have the *Shaligram*; it is
our household god. Having seen the *Shaligram* everywhere, I had
thought it alone reigned supreme. And having given up the
Shaligram and the worship of Kali and Durga, I thought we had
done with idolatry. But now I saw there were many idols such as
Agni, Vayu, Indra, Surya, etc., who had no hands and feet and
bodies, yet were perceptible by senses. Their power was felt by all.
The Vaidiks believed that if these were not propitiated all creation
would be destroyed by excess or want of rain, by the fierce heat of
the sun, or the tempestuous whirlwind. In their propitiation lay
the well-being of the universe; in their wrath its destruction.
Hence Agni, Vayu, Indra, and Surya are worshipped as gods in
the Vedas. Kali, Durga, Rama, Krishna, are all modern divinities
of the Tantras and Puranas. Agni, Vayu, Indra, and Surya, these
are the ancient Vedic gods, and the pomp and circumstance of
sacrifice concern them alone. Therefore I was obliged to give up

altogether the hope or propagating the worship of Brahma by means of the Vedas which sanction the *Karmakanda* . . .[15]

But even the Vedic sages also were far from being satisfied in their hearts with sacrificing to such finite deities as Agni, Vayu, etc. In their midst also arose the question, Where did these gods come from? The mystery of the universe began to be seriously discussed amongst them. They said, 'Who knows for certain whence came this wondrous creation? Who has ever told us here whence all these things were born? The gods were born after the creation; then who knows from whom this universe has sprung?'. . .

Then they fervently expressed themselves in this hymn of the Rigveda. Before creation 'there was then neither death nor immortal life. There was no day and night, neither was there knowledge. Then that One alone existed, animated by His own power. Naught existed but Him, this present universe was not.'[16]

Brahma Knowledge

Tagore's sole aim and object was to propagate knowledge of Brahma as taught in the Upanishads for the ultimate good of India.

When I found the knowledge of Brahma and a system of His worship in the Upanishads, and when I came to know that this was the *shastra* whose authority was recognised throughout the whole of India, I resolved to propagate the Brāhma form of worship by means of the Upanishads. All our theologians revere the Upanishads as the Vedanta, the crowning point and essence of all the Vedas. If I could preach the Brāhma Dharma as based upon the Vedanta, then all India would have one religion, all dissensions would come to an end, all would be united in a common brotherhood, her former valour and power would be revived, and finally she would regain her freedom. Such were the lofty aspirations which my mind then entertained. Idolatry with all its pomp and circumstance was to be found chiefly in the Tantras and Puranas,[17] and had no place in the Vedanta. If every one were to turn from the Tantras and Puranas to the Upanishads, if they sought to acquire the knowledge of Brahma as taught in the Upanishads, and devoted themselves to His worship, then it would result in the utmost good of India.[18]

Response to Missionary Activity

I went about in a carriage every day from morning till evening to
all the leading and distinguished men in Calcutta, and entreated
them to adopt measures by which Hindu children would no longer
have to attend missionary schools and might be educated in
schools of our own. Raja Radhakanta Deb and Raja Satyacharan
Ghosal on the one hand, on the other hand Ramgopal Ghose — I
went to each and all of them, and incited them all. They were all
fired by my enthusiasm. This did away with the rivalry between
the Dharma sabha and the Brāhma sabha, and all their disagree-
ment with each other. All were ranged on the same side, and tried
their best to prevent children going to Christian schools and missionaries making Christian converts. A large meeting was convened on the 13th Jaishtha, at which nearly a thousand people
assembled. It was resolved that, as missionaries had their free
schools, so we also should have a school where children would be
taught free of charge . . .

As a result of this meeting an educational institution called the
Hindu-hitārthi[19] was founded, and Raja Radhakanta Deb
Bahadur was appointed president to carry on its work.
Harimohun Sen and I became the secretaries. Babu Bhudeb
Mukhopadhaya was the first teacher appointed in this free school.
Thenceforward the tide of Christian conversion was stemmed,
and the cause of the missionaries received a serious blow.[20]

Valediction

*Tagore's farewell message to his followers, 1 January 1889, consists of
18 injunctions and principles of both a religious and ethical nature, the
first four of which are cited below. Injunctions 5 – 18 refer to the need
to love one's neighbour, restrain anger, do no evil, practise righteousness, abjure sinful acts, protect the Dharma and love God.*

Dearly Beloved Brethren —

Be ye united together; speak ye in unity; united know ye each
the heart of the other.

As the gods of old with one mind received each his due offering, even so be ye of one mind!

Harmonious may your efforts be, and harmonious your
thoughts and hearts,

That beauteous Peace may dwell in your midst.

Live ye all one in heart and speech.

This loving blessing and benediction, which I have just expressed in Vedic words, it is meet ye should keep well in view in the midst of the world's wranglings and jars. If to this end ye follow the way, then shall ye become gainers of your end. This way is the way of unity. If ye follow this way, all contentions shall depart from amongst you, Peace shall reign, and the Brāhma religion shall have triumph.

1. The Brāhma religion is a spiritual religion. Its seed-truth is this — By the soul shalt thou know the Supreme Soul. When God is seen in the soul, then, indeed, is He seen everywhere. The dearest dwelling-place of Him who is the root of all this complexity, the One Sovereign of all this universe, is the soul of man. If ye know not the soul, then all is empty. The soul is the root of the knowlege of God.

2. In this body dwells the soul; and within it, in the pure refulgence of spiritual consciousness, the pure, bodyless Supreme Soul is to be seen. With mind and body subdued, detached from all outward things, even-minded in sorrow and joy, self-contained, the Supreme Soul may be contemplated. This is spiritual union. When with love ye are united in this spiritual union, ye shall be delivered from all sin and shall attain the steps of salvation. After death, the body will be left here; but, united in this spiritual union, the soul shall dwell with the Soul Supreme for ever.

3. As for the health of the body ye partake of your regular daily meals, so for the soul's health the worship of God must be performed every day. The worship of God is the food of the soul.

4. 'Loving Him and doing those deeds which are pleasing in His sight, this, indeed, is His worship.' That Brahma, who is beyond Time and Space, and who yet pervades Time and Space, the Witness of all, Truth, Wisdom, and Infinity — knowing Him to be the Soul's Ruler and the Heart's Lord, adore Him every day with love; and, for the good of the world, busy yourself in the performance of those works of righteousness which are pleasing in his sight. Never dissever these two ever-united limbs of God's worship.[21]

NOTES

1 Kalighat: the temple of Kali in Calcutta.
2 *The Autobiography of Maharshi Devendranath Tagore*, (London, 1914), 49 – 51.
3 Ibid., 42.
4 Ibid., 96 – 7.
5 Ibid., 280.
6 Ibid., 251 – 3.
7 i.e., the doctrines of Monism, Incarnation, and Illusion.
8 *Autobiography*, 165, 175 – 6.
9 Tatwabodhini Sabha: an association founded 1 October 1839 by Devendran̄ath Tagore to gain knowledge of God.
10 *Autobiography*, 66, 76 – 8.
11 Durga Puja: the principal religious festival in Bengal.
12 Ashwin: September – October.
13 Rammoni Thakur: father of Dwārkanāth Tagore.
14 *Autobiography*, 55 – 6.
15 Karmakanda: ceremonial rights and observances.
16 *The Autobiography*, 135 – 7.
17 The Puranas are Scriptures later than the Vedas. They are a storehouse of mythological and historical legends, and also the popular *shashtras* or sacred books in everyday use. Tantras represent an esoteric phase of Hinduism, generally later than that of the Puranas.
18 *Autobiography*, 102 – 3.
19 Hindu-hitārthi: the well-wisher of Hindus.
20 *Autobiography*, 100 – 1.
21 Ibid., 290 – 1.

REFERENCE

The Autobiography of Maharshi Devendranath Tagore. Translated from the original Bengali by Satyendranath Tagore and Indira Devi. Introduction by Evelyn Underhill. London: Macmillan, 1914.

3

KESHUB CHUNDER SEN (1838 – 1884)

Initiated into the Brahmo Samāj by Devendranāth Tagore, Sen's unbounded enthusiasm and vitality proved a mixed blessing to the society which ultimately became fragmented into the Adi Brahmo Samāj led by Tagore, the Brahmo Samāj of India founded by Sen and the Sādāran Brahmo Samāj set up by Sen's disenchanted followers.

Sen was born into a well-to-do-family in Calcutta renowned for its culture and openness to Western influences. Educated at the Hindu College he took a great interest in Western philosophy and established the Sangut Sabha, a goodwill fraternity for the discussion of contemporary issues. He was attracted to the Brahmo Samāj from his reading of a tract relating to the society and in 1859, as a result of the personal interest taken in him by Devendranāth Tagore, he became joint secretary of the Samāj. His enthusiasm to propagate the message of the society led him to found the *Indian Mirror* and the *Dharmatattva*, two new journals of religion and philosophy, to undertake a lecture tour through Bombay, Poona and Madras, and to preach sermons, write tracts and establish schools. His eloquent and powerful advocacy of the society's ideals ensured the formation of Samājes in many parts of India and it was as a result of his efforts that the society became a nationwide movement.

Sen was committed to religious and social reform and his radicalism in this respect opened up a gulf between him and Tagore. His rejection of caste, child marriages and purdah, and his promotion of the remarriage of widows and the education of women, put him in the forefront of Indian social reform. In 1865 the differences between him and other members of the Brahmo Samāj were sufficiently acute to occasion the formation of the Brahmo Samāj of India. A further schism occurred as a result of the marriage of his daughter before the prescribed marriageable age to the Maharaja of Kuch Bihar. Sen claimed the marriage to be in accordance with God's will but his dissident followers objected to his inspirational claims and in 1878 founded the Sādhāran Brahmo Samāj.

Among the influences on Sen during his life was that of Rāmakrishna and Christianity. Under the influence of the former he accepted the symbolic significance of many Hindu rituals and practices and discarding his fear of image-worship came to recognize that the Hindu pantheon was only an expression of the different ways ordinary Hindus sought to satisfy their desire for a tangible Deity and manifest their love and reverence for God. Christianity provided him with some of the terminology used to express the principles of the New Dispensation which he proclaimed in 1879. He refers to it as a gospel and a church; as on the same level as the Jewish and Christian dispensations; as the fulfilment of Christ's prophecy; as the harmonization of all scriptures and all religions; and as a message of love which proscribed every distinction between Brahmans and Sūdras, Asiatics and Europeans. Its universal character is illustrated by his description of it as 'the celestial court where around enthroned Divinity shine the lights of all heavenly saints and prophets'. Its uniqueness for him lay in its insistence on direct worship with no mediator between God and man.

Sen's acceptance of the divinity of Christ, his description of himself as Jesudas, the servant of Jesus, and remarks such as 'Christ rules India', suggest that he had completely embraced the Christian faith. But for him Christ is an Asiatic and his divinity the divinity of humanity, an essentially Hindu doctrine. His life and character is in accordance with the ideal of Hindu life and his concept of oneness with God is comparable with the Vedāntic notion of man's identity with the Godhead. His concept of incarnation is not the embodiment of the absolute perfection of divinity but the manifestation of God in humanity, God *in* mankind rather than God *made* man. God reveals himself in history through great men, and prophets are divine incarnations in the sense that they manifest the spirit of God.

Sen's acceptance of the providential nature of British rule in India is in accordance with the general climate of opinion of the time but it did not prevent him from specifically criticizing that section of the European community which delighted in vilifying native customs and manners. Deliberate misrepresentation and uncharitable treatment of the native population did nothing to enhance the reputation of the British who, in Sen's view, would do well to study the ancient literature of India and learn from the wisdom of the rishis.

Sen's contribution to the development of Indian thought was important not so much for the consistency of his teaching as for the enthusiasm, eloquence and emotional intensity he brought to propagating the ideals of the Brahmo Samāj and the Brahmo Samāj of India.

KESHUB CHUNDER SEN

Revelation

The first manifestation of God is in nature, and it is from this that
the earliest religious impressions of men and nations have been
derived. This is the primary and ordinary revelation of God, and
one which is accessible and intelligible to all alike. Man, in the
simplicity of his uneducated mind, and without the aid of logic or
philosophy, 'traces nature up to nature's God'. He cannot but do
so.

The universe exhibits on all sides innumerable marks of design
and beauty, of adaptation and method, which he cannot explain
except by referring them to an Intelligent First Cause, the Creator
of this vast universe . . . But is God manifest in the universe
simply as its Maker — who created it, but has no connection
whatever with it at present? Does the universe bear the same relation to God as the watch does to the watchmaker? Certainly not.
The world cannot exist for one moment without God. He is its life
and power. . .

There is another revelation; there is *God in History*. He who
created and upholds this vast universe also governs the destinies
and affairs of nations . . . But in what manner does God manifest
Himself in history? Through great men . . . They are great on
account of the large measure of divine spirit they possess and
manifest. It is true they are men; but who will deny that they are
above ordinary humanity? Though human, they are divine . . . I
look upon a prophet as a divine incarnation; in this sense, that he
is the spirit of God manifest in human flesh. True incarnation is
not, as popular theology defines it, the absolute perfection of the
divine nature embodied in mortal form; it is not the God of the
universe putting on a human body — the infinite becoming finite
in space and time, in intelligence and power. It simply means God
manifest in humanity; — not God made man, but God *in* man.[1]

Jesus Christ

Asiatic

If, however, our Christian friends persist in traducing our nationality and in distrusting and hating Orientalism, let me assure them
that I do not in the least feel dishonoured by such imputations.

On the contrary, I rejoice, yea, I am proud, that I am an Asiatic. And was not Jesus Christ an Asiatic? (Deafening applause.) Yes, and his disciples were Asiatics, and all the agencies primarily employed for the propagation of the gospel were Asiatic. In fact, Christianity was founded and developed by Asiatics, and in Asia. When I reflect on this, my love for Jesus becomes a hundredfold intensified; I feel him nearer my heart, and deeper in my national sympathies. Why should I then feel ashamed to acknowledge that nationality which he acknowledged? . . . In Christ we see not only the· exaltedness of humanity, but also the grandeur of which Asiatic nature is susceptible. To us Asiatics, therefore Christ is doubly interesting, and his religion is entitled to our peculiar regard as an altogether Oriental affair. The more this great fact is pondered, the less I hope will be the antipathy and hatred of European Christians against Oriental nationalities, and the greater the interest of the Asiatics in the teachings of Christ.[2]

Recall to your minds, gentlemen, the true Asiatic Christ, divested of all Western appendages, carrying on the work of redemption among his own people. Behold, he cometh to us in his loose flowing garment, his dress and features altogether oriental, a perfect Asiatic in everything.[3]

Divinity

Verily there is such a thing as divinity in Christ. But what is this divinity? . . .

It appears to me that Christ held earnestly and consistently what I should, in the absence of a better expression, call the doctrine of divine humanity . . . Christ struck the keynote of his doctrine when he announced his divinity before an astonished and amazed world in these words: 'I and my Father are one.' . . . These words clearly mean . . . nothing more than the highest form of self-denial . . . He had his life rooted in Divinity. He felt always that the Lord was underlying his whole existence . . . To manifest this divine life in humanity was his mission, and the unvarying burden of his exhortations.[4]

Pre-existence

As an Idea, as a plan of life, as a predetermined dispensation yet to be realised, as parity of character, not concrete but abstract, as

light not yet manifested. That was the form in which Christ dwelt
from all eternity in the bosom of the Father. Looking at himself in
this light Christ could not but believe in his pre-existence . . .
Though the human Christ was born, all that was divine in him
existed eternally in God.[5]

Incarnation

There is an uncreated Christ, as also the created Christ, the idea
of the son and the incarnate son drawing all his vitality and
inspiration from the Father. This is the true doctrine of the incarnation. Take away from Christ all that is divine, all that is God's,
no Christ remains . . . He taught only one doctrine — divinity in
humanity.[6]

You will find on reflection that the doctrine of divine humanity
is essentially a Hindu doctrine, and the picture of Christ's life and
character I have drawn is altogether a picture of ideal Hindu life.
Surely, the idea of absorption and immersion in the Deity is one
of those ideas of Vedantic Hinduism which prevail extensively in
India. From the highest sage to the humblest peasant, millions of
men in this land believe in the pantheistic doctrine of man's identity with the Godhead.[7]

The incarnations (Avatara) come and go finishing the work en-
trusted to them, but the world does not know that they survive
their allotted span of life. Their material forms change but the
divine in them lasts for ever; inasmuch as an incarnation means
the manifestation of some special attribute or attributes of God
brought to a focus.[8]

Sonship

Honour Christ, but never be 'Christian' in the popular accepta-
tion of the term. Christ is not Christianity. In accepting the
former take care you do not accept the latter. Let it be your ambition to outgrow the popular types of narrow Christian faith, and
merge in the vastness of Christ. Neither should you become
'Christian', nor should you simply aspire to be 'Christlike', for
then you would represent the lower strata of spiritual life.
Advance to a higher ideal, my friends. Be Christ . . . For what is
Christ? Not a doctrine, but the eternal and universal spirit of son-
ship.[9]

Future Church

The future church will uphold the absolute infinity and unity of
the Divine Creator, and will suffer no created thing or being to
usurp His sovereignty. It will worship Him alone and thoroughly
set its face against every form of creature worship.[10]

But the future church of India must be thoroughly national; it
must be an essentially Indian Church. The future religion of the
world I have described will be the common religion of all nations,
but in each nation it will have an indigenous growth, and assume a
distinctive and peculiar character. All mankind will unite in a
universal church; at the same time, it will be adapted to the
peculiar circumstances of each nation, and assume a national
form . . . India has religious traditions and associations, tastes
and customs, peculiarly sacred and dear to her, just as every other
country has, and it is idle to expect that she will forgo these; nay,
she cannot do so, as they are interwoven with her very life. In
common with all other nations and communities, we shall
embrace the theistic worship, creed, and gospel of the future
church — we shall acknowledge and adore the Holy One, accept
the love and service of God and man as our creed, and put our
firm faith in God's almighty grace as the only means of our
redemption. But we shall do all this in a strictly national and
Indian style.[11]

The New Dispensation

What I accept as the New Dispensation in India neither shuts out
God's light from the rest of the world, nor does it run counter to
any of those marvellous dispensations of His mercy which were
made in ancient times. It only shows a new adaptation of His eternal goodness, an Indian version and application of His universal
love.[12]

Is this new gospel a Dispensation, or is it simply a new system
of religion, which human understanding has evolved? I say it
stands upon the same level with the Jewish dispensation, the
Christian dispensation, and the Vaishnava dispensation through
Chaitanya. It is a divine Dispensation, fully entitled to a place
among the various dispensations and revelations of the world.[13]

My individuality is lost in the community that forms my
Church. This dispensation will not tolerate any form of egotism.

It hides me in my brother-apostles . . . We are lost in each other, and all distinctive personality is emerged in the unity of the common Church . . . While other dispensations have their special mediatorial agencies between God and a sinful world, here we have no such thing, no intercessor, no mediator . . . Upon every theist the new gospel imposes the inviolable vow of direct worship. This is the peculiarity of the present dispensation, and in this, more perhaps than in anything else, it differs from all other dispensations.[14]

Besides immediacy there is another characteristic of the present dispensation which distinguishes it from all other religions. It is inclusive, while they are more or less exclusive. They exclude each other. But this includes all religions. This dispensation shuns altogether the old-path exclusivism, and establishes for itself the new character of an all-embracing and all-absorbing eclecticism. No one can be true to the New Dispensation who indulges in sectarian hatred and bigotry, and lives in a strait church which excludes the rest of the world.[15]

We are the fulfilment of Moses. He was simply the incarnation of Divine conscience. But there was no science in his teachings, that science which in modern times is so greatly honoured. Let Moses grow into modern science, and you have the New Dispensation, which may be characterized as the union of conscience and science. As for Christ, we are surely among his honoured ambassadors. We are a deduction and corollary from his teachings. The New Dispensation is Christ's prophecy fulfilled.[16]

Paul was raised by God to break caste, and level the distinctions of race and nationality; and nobly did he fulfil his mission. The Jew and the Gentile he made into one body. The modern Pauls of the New Dispensation are carrying on a similar crusade against caste in India. The obnoxious distinctions between Brahmin and Sudra, between Hindu and Yavana, between Asiatic and European, the new gospel of love thoroughly proscribes . . . In this anti-caste movement, which daily brings Jew and Gentile, Hindu and Christian, nearer and nearer in spriritual fellowship, the chief workers are verily spiritual descendants of Moses, Jesus, and Paul.[17]

Such is the New Dispensation. It is the harmony of all scriptures and prophets and dispensations. It is not an isolated creed, but the science which binds and explains and harmonizes all religions. It gives to history a meaning, to the action of Providence a consistency, to quarrelling churches a common bond, and to successive dispensations a continuity. It shows marvellous synthesis how the different rainbow colours are one in the light of heaven. The New Dispensation is the sweet music of diverse instruments. It is the precious necklace in which are strung together the rubies and pearls of all ages and climes. It is the celestial court where around enthroned Divinity shine the lights of all heavenly saints and prophets. It is the wonderful solvent, which fuses all dispensations into a new chemical compound. It is the mighty absorbent, which absorbs all that is true and good and beautiful in the objective world. Before the flag of the New Dispensation bow ye nations, and proclaim the Fatherhood of God and the Brotherhood of man.[18]

Religions

History also shows us that no religious system recorded therein is wholly false. Millions of men worship birds, beasts, and reptiles, but their creeds, if closely analysed, will show many redeeming features. However superstitious their practices and objectionable their doctrines, as there is no absolute truth, so there is no absolute falsehood in them. As in men, so in systems of philosophy and theology, we see nowhere unmixed purity or impurity. We must not, therefore, pronounce indiscriminate condemnation upon any creed, nor cherish sectarian antipathy towards its followers. We should distinguish what is true in it from its false administers, and in a liberal spirit note the power features common to all creeds.[19]

There are some among us who denounce Mohamedanism as wholly false, while others contend that Hinduism is altogether false. Such opinions are far from being correct; they only indicate the spirit of sectarian antipathy . . . There is, no doubt, in each of these creeds, much to excite to ridicule, and perhaps indignation in a large amount of superstition, prejudice, and even corruption. But I must emphatically say it is wrong to set down Hinduism or Mohamedanism as nothing but a mass of lies and abominations, and worthy of being trampled under foot. Proscribe and eliminate all that is false therein: there remains a residue of truth and priority which you are bound to honour.[20]

Idols

India, you know, has always sought a visible Divinity, and for centuries knelt at the feet of millions of idols of her own creation. The vast and varied parthenon of the Hindu theology, which has degraded the nation and paralyzed its religious spirit, indicates only the countless ways in which the Hindu mind has always striven to satisfy its intense craving after a visible and tangible Deity.[21]

It may seem strange, yet nevertheless it is true, that even the curse of idolatry has proved a blessing to us. To the myriad gods and goddesses of India, to the Mahabharata, the Ramayana, and all the legends of Hindu mythology we owe a debt of gratitude. It is these divinities, however unreal, that have called forth the varied affections of the Hindu mind. The worshippers of Rama and Krishna, whatever their errors, have worshipped their gods with hearts full of devotional feelings. The devoted Vaishnava lives in the midst of an overflow of deep sentiments. Personal feelings towards a visible and personal divinity, the warmest sentiments of gratitude, the sweetest feelings of love, filial tenderness and friendly communion, abound in the heart of the Hindu idolator. And this exuberance of devotional sentiments our Puranic ancestors have taught us. Their errors and prejudices we pity, their idolatry and superstition we shun as darkness, but their intense love, reverence, and faith we gratefully honour and imitate.[22]

The British

I cannot but reflect with grateful interest on the day when the British nation first planted their feet on the plains of India, and the successive steps by which the British Empire has been established and consolidated in this country. It is to the British Government that we owe our deliverance from oppression and misrule, from darkness and distress, from ignorance and superstition. Those enlightened ideas which have changed the very life of the nation, and have gradually brought about such wondrous improvement in native society, are the gifts of that Government; and so likewise the inestimable boon of freedom of thought and action, which we so justly prize. Are not such considerations calculated to rouse our deepest gratitude and loyalty to the British nation and Her Most Gracious Majesty Queen Victoria?[23]

Among the European community in India there is a class who not only hate the Natives with their whole heart, but seem to take pleasure in doing so. (Cheers.) The existence of such a class of men cannot possibly be disputed. They regard the Natives as one of the vilest nations on earth, hopelessly immersed in all the vices which can degrade humanity, and bring it to the level of the brutes. They think it mean even to associate with the Natives. Native ideas and tastes, Native customs and manners, seem to them odious and contemptible; while Native character is considered to represent the lowest type of lying and wickedness . . . To say the least, I hold this to be a most uncharitable misrepresentation. (Hear, hear.) I believe, and I must boldly and emphatically declare, that the heart of a Native is not naturally more depraved than that of a European or any other nation in the world.[24]

Many a European adventurer in this country seems to believe that he has a right to trample upon every unfortunate nigger with whom he comes in contact. (Cheers.) This he believes to be heroism, and in this he seeks glory! But he forgets that to kick and trample upon one who is inferior in strength is not heroism, but base cowardice. (Deafening applause.) . . . If the European is at all anxious for the glory of his country and his God, he ought to seek it in a better and more generous treatment of the Natives.[25]

Loyalty shuns an impersonal abstraction. It demands a person, and that person is the sovereign, or the head of the state, in whom law and constitution are visibly typified and represented. We are right then if our loyalty means not only respect for law and the Parliament, but personal attachment to Victoria, Queen of England and Empress of India . . . Do you not recognize the finger of providence in the progress of nations? Assuredly the record of British rule in India is not a chapter of profane history, but of eccesiastical history. (Cheers.) The book which treats of the moral, social, and religious advancement of our great country with the help of Western science, under the paternal rule of the British nation, is indeed a sacred book. There we see clearly that it is Providence that rules India through England. (Applause.) . . . Who can deny that Victoria is an instrument in the hands of Providence to elevate this degraded country in the scale of nations, and that in her hands the solemn trust has lately been most solemnly reposed? Glory then, to Empress Victoria! (Applause.)[26]

NOTES

1　*Keshub Chunder Sen's Lectures in India*, (London, 1901), 52 – 61.
2　Ibid., 33 – 4.
3　Ibid., 365.
4　Ibid., 367 – 73.
5　Ibid., 375 – 6.
6　Ibid., 379.
7　Ibid., 386 – 7.
8　*Sadhusamagama: Discourses on Pilgrimage to Prophets*, (Calcutta, n.d.), 72.
9　*Lectures in India*, 488 – 9.
10　Ibid., 143.
11　Ibid., 158 – 9.
12　Ibid., 198.
13　Ibid., 447 – 8.
14　Ibid., 452 – 3.
15　Ibid., 456 – 7.
16　Ibid., 465.
17　Ibid., 467 – 8.
18　Ibid., 490 – 1.
19　Ibid., 133.
20　Ibid., 155.
21　Ibid., 205.
22　Ibid., 255 – 6.
23　Ibid., 20.
24　Ibid., 22 – 3.
25　Ibid., 30.
26　Ibid., 322 – 4.

REFERENCES

Keshub Chunder Sen's Lectures in India. London: Cassell, 1901.
Keshub Chunder Sen, *Sadhusamagama: Discourses on Pilgrimage to Prophets*. Translated by Jamini Kanto Koar. Calcutta: Navavidhan Publication Committee, n.d.

4

DAYĀNANDA SARASWATĪ (1824 – 1883)

One of the most influential figures in the history of modern India, Dayānanda has been rightly described as a rugged individualist. From his early youth to the end of his life he determined his own course of action and took his own decisions. If this attitude made for originality of thought it also prompted accusations of arrogance and autocratic behaviour and led to people being alienated from him. But this did not deter him in any way from his search for truth.

Although he refused to divulge the names of his parents or his birthplace in his autobiography it is generally believed that he was born in Tankara in the small state of Morvi. His father was a brahmin landowner whose occupation involved tax-collecting and money-lending. He saw to it, as a devout Śaivite, that his son was properly instructed in religious rituals and caste customs. At the age of ten Dayānanda was initiated into the daily worship of the *linga*, the phallic symbol of Śiva, and four years later taken to the Śivarātri temple ceremony which included fasting and an all-night vigil. While others slept Dayānanda remained awake to witness mice polluting the emblem of Śiva and consuming the food offerings. His doubts and misgivings about the desecration that he had witnessed were not allayed by his father's explanation about the representational character of the emblem with the result that his antipathy to idol worship grew leading eventually to his abstinence from regular temple worship. The death of his younger sister from cholera made him reflect on the brevity of life and its ultimate aim — mokṣa. In order to change the content and direction of this thinking his parents pressed him to consider marriage and proceeded to make arrangements along those lines. To avoid this Dayānanda left home and began the quest for truth that was to last for the rest of his life.

He was initiated as a sannyāsī in the order of the Dandīs by Purnānanda Sarasvatī who gave him the name by which he is known. His quest for truth and for the perfect guru who would show him the way to mokṣa took him to holy places of pilgrimage throughout northern India but all to no avail. In 1860 he arrived at Mathura where he studied Sanskrit for three years with the blind guru Virjānanda Sarasvatī and on his departure promised to propagate the books of the rishis and the Vedic religion. From this time on his quest for individual liberation was replaced by a concern for the regeneration of Hinduism and the solitary sannyāsī became a public preacher and teacher.

Dayānanda's antipathy to idol worship finds expression in public criticism of the superstitious beliefs and practices of Hinduism and positive instruction in Vedic rites. He had become increasingly concerned with the authoritative source of Hinduism and had concluded that Vedic revelation as contained in the four Vedas constituted the only true revelation and the source of the Hindi religion, a view he defended against Keshub Chunder Sen's more pluralist views. Through the generosity of his followers he founded schools to teach the Vedas but this proved an unsuccessful experiment. More successful was his insistence on the need for morality in true religion and his denunciation of idol worship as contrary to the teaching of the scriptures. His emphasis on high moral principles led to his outspoken letter to Maharaja Singh of Jodhpur criticizing him for his drinking, gambling and womanizing and urging him to mend his ways. Whether this outspokenness was the cause of his poisoning by one of the Maharaja's courtesans, as his followers claim, is not certain, but that he died from an illness suddenly contracted at Jodhpur is a matter of fact.

His views on social issues include those on child marriage, widow remarriage, and niyoga, the temporary legal union of widows and widowers, and the education of children, especially girls. Dayānanda was aware of the interrelation of the problems of early widowhood and child marriage and also the relation between the dowry system and female infanticide. He believed that the eradication of the practice of child marriage would reduce the number of widows but in the meantime the solution to the problem of early widowhood was to sanction niyoga. The eduction of children, including Śūdras, should involve the study of Hindi and Sanskrit as well as other languages, schools should be egalitarian catering for the instruction of boys up to the age of twenty-five and girls up to the minimum age of sixteen.

The Ārya Samāj founded by Dayānanda in Bombay in 1875 provided him with the organization necessary for the propagation of reformation ideals. The rules adopted by the society were a mixture of religious and moral beliefs and organizational details. Belief in God and the authority of the Vedas was basic. No idol could represent God nor could it be maintained that he assumed bodily form as an avatar. The duty of all members of the Samāj was to promote spiritual monotheism, Vedic authority and social

reform. The growth of the Samāj gave the movement a momen-
tum of its own which was helped by the fact that each Samāj
established became an autonomous society. Dayānanda refused
to set up a central authority or to act as president of the movement, Its success was most pronounced in Bengal where
significantly Hindu national self-consciousness was to play an
important role in the struggle for Indian independence.

Dayānanda's promotion of Hindi as a national language is not
unrelated to the development of national self-consciousness since
he was aware of the intimate connection that pertained between
language, religion and nationalism, and the fact that political
independence was the natural corollary of the restoration of Vedic
ideals. His fierce attack on Christianity for its idolatry,
mythology and barbarism, accusations more often levelled by
missionaries against Hinduism, points to the aggressive nature of
his nationalism. He is sometimes referred to as the Luther of
India compared with Rāmmohan Roy's more Erasmian
approach, and given his deep-seated desire to lead his fellow
countrymen back to the Vedas the description may not be in-
appropriate.

DAYĀNANDA SARASWATĪ

Religion

I believe in a religion based on universal and all-embracing principles which has always been accepted as true by mankind, and will continue to command the allegiance of mankind in the ages to come. Hence it is that the religion in question is called the *primeval eternal religion*, which means that it is above the hostility of all human creeds whatsoever . . .

My conception of God and all other objects in the universe is founded on the teachings of *Veda* and other true *Shastras*, and is in conformity with the beliefs of all the sages, from *Brahma* down to *Jaimini* . . . That alone I hold to be acceptable which is worthy of being believed by all men in all ages. I do not entertain the least idea of founding a new religion or sect. My sole aim is to believe in truth and help others to believe in it, to reject falsehood and help others to do the same. Had I been biased, I would have championed any one of the religions prevailing in India. But I have not done so. On the contrary, I do not approve of what is objectionable and false in the institutions of this or any other country, nor do I reject what is good and in harmony with the dictates of true religion, nor have I any desire to do so, since a contrary conduct is wholly unworthy of man.[1]

We have incorporated into this book whatever is true in all religions and in harmony with their highest teachings but have refuted whatever is false in them. We have exposed to the view of men — learned or otherwise — all evil practices whether resorted to secretly or openly. This will help our readers to discuss religious questions in a spirit of love and embrace the one true religion. Though we were born in Aryavarta (India) and still live in it, yet just as we do not defend the evil doctrines and practices of the religions prevailing in our own country — on the other hand expose them properly — in like manner we deal with alien religions. We treat foreigners in the same way as we treat our own countrymen in recognition of our common humanity. It behoves all the rest to act likewise. Had we taken the side of one of the prevailing religions of India: we would have but followed (blindly) the example of sectarians who extol, defend and preach their own religion and decry, refute and check the progress of other creeds. In our opinion, however, such things are beneath the dignity of man.[2]

Vedas

O. — What is your faith?

A. — *Vedic*. We believe that the *Vedas* alone are the supreme authority in the ascertainment of true religion — the *true conduct of life*. What is enjoined by the *Vedas* we hold to be right; whilst whatever is condemned by them we believe to be wrong. Therefore we say that our religion is *Vedic*. All men, especially the Aryas, should believe in the *Vedas* and thereby cultivate unity in religion.[3]

I hold that the four *Vedas* — the repository of Knowledge and Religious Truths — are the Word of God. They comprise what is known as the *Sanhita* — *Mantra* portion only. They are absolutely free from error, and are an authority unto themselves. In other words, they do not stand in need of any other book to uphold their authority. Just as the sun (or a lamp) by its light, reveals its own nature as well as that of other objects of the universe, such as the earth — even so are the *Vedas*.[4]

Had He revealed the Veda in the language of some particular country, He would have been partial to that country, because it would have been easier for the people of that country to learn and teach the *Veda* than for the foreigners, therefore, it is that He did it in *Sanskrit* that belongs to no country, and is the mother of all languages.[5]

I preach *Vedic* truths. I am thus a preacher and do not wish to be anything more than this. You (Theosophists) call me some time member, some time something else. I do not wish to be honoured or have any high position (in any organisation).[6]

Idols

During the Shivaratri vigil Dayānanda witnessed a mouse climbing on the idol of Shiva and eating the akshata (offerings).

I awoke my father and asked him to tell me whether the hideous emblem of Shiva in the temple was identical with the Mahadeva of the scriptures? Why do you ask this? enquired my father. I feel it is impossible, I replied, to reconcile to the idea of an omnipotent, living god, with this idol which allows the mice to run over his body and thus suffers his image to be polluted without the slightest protest.

My father tried to explain to me that this stone representation of the Mahadeva of Kailash, having been consecrated by the holy men, became in consequence the god himself, and is worshipped and regarded as such. As Shiva cannot be perceived, he further added, in this *Kaliyuga*, we have the idol in which the Mahadeva of Kailash is imagined by his votaries. This kind of worship pleases the great deity as much as if instead of the emblem he were there himself. But the explanation fell short of satisfying me. I could not help suspecting misinterpretation and sophistry in all this.[7]

God being Formless and Omnipresent cannot have an image. If the sight of an idol puts God in one's mind why cannot this wonderful creation which comprehends the earth, water, fire, air, and vegetation and a hundred and one other things? . . .

Being All-pervading He cannot be imagined to exist in any particular object only.[8]

True happiness consists solely in giving up altogether the worship of idols and in serving another and other living gods. It is an awful shame that people should have given up the worship of the living gods that impart happiness and have taken to the worship of idols instead . . .

It is evil practices like idol worship that are responsible for the existence of millions of idle, lazy, indolent, and beggarly priests in India, who are mainly answerable for this widespread ignorance, fraud and mendacity in the country.[9]

O. — Idol-worship and pilgrimage to holy places have been in vogue since time immemorial. How can they be false?

A. — What do you call *time immemorial*? If you say that by the use of these words you mean that these practices have *always* been in vogue it cannot be right, otherwise how would you account for the fact that there is no mention of these things in the *Vedas*, the *Brahmanas* and other ancient books of sages and seers. The practice of worshipping idols originated with the *Vama Margis* and the Jainees a little under 2,000 or 2,500 years back. It did not exist in India in ancient times, nor were there any *places held sacred* (*tirathas*) then.[10]

God, Soul, Prakriti

He, Who is called *Brahma*, or the most High; who is *Paramatma* or the Supreme Spirit Who permeates the whole universe; Who is a true personification of Existence, Consciousness and Bliss;

Whose nature, attributes and characteristics are Holy; Who is
Omniscient, Formless, All-pervading, Unborn, Infinite,
Almighty, Just and Merciful; Who is the author of the universe
and sustains and dissolves it; Who awards all souls the fruits of
their deeds in strict accordance with the requirements of absolute
justice and is possessed of the like attributes, even *Him* I believe
to be the Great God.[11]

O. — There are more gods than one mentioned in the *Vedas*.
Do you believe this or not?

A. — No, we do not; as nowhere in all the four *Vedas* there is
written anything that could go to show that there are more gods
than one. On the other hand, it is clearly said in many places that
there is only one god.[12]

O. — Does God incarnate or not?

A. — No; because it is said in the *Yajur Veda* 'He is unborn'
again 'He overspreads all. He is pure, is never born and never
takes on a human form.' It is clear from these quotations that god
is never born.[13]

The doctrine of the incarnation of God cannot stand even the
test of reasoning, for He, who pervades the universe like ether, is
Infinite, Invisible, and is not susceptible to pleasure and pain,
cannot be contained in a drop of semen or in the uterus or in a
bodily tenement.[14]

Similarly, both the *soul* and the *material cause* of this universe,
being pervaded by *God*, never were, nor are, nor shall ever be
separate from Him, and being in their natures *distinct* from Him
can ever be *one* with Him. The *Vedantists* of today are like one-
eyed men who see only one side of the street they pass through
and are bent on giving such a great importance to the *close connection* or *relationship* between God and the soul that they completely ignore the *dissimilitudes* between the two.[15]

God and the soul are distinct entities, being different in nature
and characteristics: they are, however, inseparable being related
as the pervader and the pervaded and having certain attributes in
common. Just as a material object has never been and shall never
be, separable from the space in which it exists; nor has it ever been
or shall ever be one and the same or identical with it; even so, I
hold that God and the souls are related as the pervader and the
pervaded, worshipped and worshipper, father and son, and
having other similar relations . . .

There are three things beginningless: namely, God, Souls, and *Prakriti* or the material cause of the universe. These are also ever-existing. As they are eternal, their attributes, works and nature are also eternal.[16]

The *Neo-Vedantists* look upon God as the *efficient* as well as the *material* cause of the universe, but they are absolutely in the wrong.[17]

Moksha

Moksha or salvation is the emancipation of the soul from all woes and sufferings, and to live bondfree, a life of liberty and free movement in the all-pervading God and His creation, and resumption of the earthly life after the expiration of a fixed period of enjoying salvation.[18]

O. — Is the soul in *Emancipation* absorbed into God or does it retain its individuality?

A. — It retains its separate individuality, for should it get absorbed into the Divine Spirit, who would then enjoy the bliss of *Emancipation* . . . Absorption of the soul into the Divine Spirit is not *Emancipation* but its death or *annihilation*.[19]

With regard to *Emancipation* as *absorption into God* it is like death by drowning oneself into the sea.[20]

Social Reforms

Caste

I hold that the *varna* (caste or class or order of an individual) is determined by his merits (qualifications) and action.[21]

When the *Kshatriyas* and others who had more money than brains become their dupes, these so called *Brahmans* got a golden opportunity of enjoying sensual pleasures ad libitum. They also declared that all the best things of the earth were meant for the *Brahmans* only. In other words, they subverted the whole system of *Classes* and *Orders*, and based it on the mere accident of birth, instead of on the qualifications, character and works of the people, as it originally was.[22]

All individuals should be placed in different *Classes* according to the qualifications, accomplishments and character. By adopting this system all will advance in every respect, because the higher *Classes* will be in constant fear of their children being degraded to the *Shudra Class*, if they are not properly educated. The same fear will also make the children acquire knowledge and culture. Whilst the lower *Classes* will be stimulated to exert themselves for admission into the *Classes* above them.[23]

Women

Now if the husbands be well educated and the wife ignorant or *vice versa*, there will be a constant state of warfare in the house. Besides if women were not to study, where will the teachers, for Girls' schools come from? Nor could ever the affairs of state, the administration of justice, and the duties of married life, that are required of both husband and wife . . . be carried on properly without thorough education (of men and women) . . . Therefore it behoves *Brahman* and *Kshatriya* women to acquire all kinds of knowledge, and *Vaishya* women to learn trade, and the mechanical arts and the like, and *Shudra* women, the art of cooking, etc. As men should, at the very least, learn the Science of Grammar, *Dharma* and their profession or trade, likewise should women learn Grammar, *Dharma*, Medical Science, Mathematics and the mechanical and fine arts at the least, for without a knowledge of these, ascertainment of truth, proper behaviour towards their husbands and other people, bearing of good children, their proper upbringing and instruction, proper management of the household affairs, preparation of foods and drinks in accordance with the requirements of Medical Science, . . . can never be effected.[24]

Let the husband and the wife whenever they separate from or meet each other for the first time during the day or the night, greet each other with *hamastey* which means, *I respect you.*[25]

Marriage

The best form of marriage is *that by choice* (Swayamvara), after the education of the contracting parties is finished and their *Brahmacharya* for the aforesaid periods completed. Happy is the country wherein the people devote themselves to the pursuit of knowledge, live chaste lives, and adopt the aforesaid form of marriage.[26]

The *Swaymvara marriage*, i.e. marriage by choice — the most ancient form of marriage in India — is the best form of marriage. Before a man and maid think of marrying, they should see that they suit each other in point of knowledge, disposition, character, beauty, age, strength, family, stature, and build of body and the like. Until they suit each other in all these things, no happiness can result from marriage. Nor can marriage in early life ever lead to any beneficial result.[27]

Remarriage

Says the sage *Manu* on this subject, 'A man or a women, who has simply gone through the ceremony of *joining hands* but whose marriage has not been consummated, is entitled to re-marry.'

But remarriage is absolutely prohibited in the case of a twice-born man or women (ie, one belonging to a *Brahman, Kshatriya* or *Vaishya Class*) who has had sexual intercourse with his or her consort.[28]

Niyoga

Niyoga is the temporary union of a person with another of the opposite sex, of the same or higher class, as a measure in exceptional or distressing conditions, for the raising of issue in widowhood, or when he or she is suffering from some permanent disease, like impotence or sterility.[29]

A married couple can produce children up to the limit of ten, while that connected by *Niyoga* cannot produce more than two or four.

Just as marriage is allowed only in the case of a bachelor and a maid, likewise only a widow and a widower can enter into the relation of *Niyoga*, but never a bachelor and a maid.

A married couple always lives together but not that connected by *Niyoga*. Such persons should come together only when they intend to *generate a new life*.[30]

Education

Letter from Dayānanda to Col. Alcott, Moradabad, 13 July 1879

With regard to your proposal of translating *Veda bhashya* into English and then publishing it in your Journal, I am of the opinion that it is an uphill task to translate faithfully one language into another . . . Supposing all these arrangements can be successfully made, the greatest drawback then is that the English-knowing people of India will on the appearance of the English translation of my *Vedabhashya* give up the Sanskrit and Hindi studies which they are so vehemently pursuing nowadays in order to enable themselves to read the *Vedabhashya*. This (popularising Sanskrit and Hindi) is the chief object of mine . . . It is, however, not my desire to prohibit you from translating this work, for without the English translation, the European nations cannot catch the true light. But first consider the above point.[31]

Letter from Dayānanda to Nirbhe Ram, Ajmer, 23 May 1881

In your school (Farrukhabad), Sanskrit is getting very scant attention, whereas other languages, English, Urdu, Persian, etc. are cared more. It shows that the school does not satisfy the aim for which it was opened and thousands of rupees are going waste as far as propagation of Sanskrit is concerned . . . Sanskrit is being neglected everywhere . . .

English is becoming people's mother tongue now and it is being taught quite effectively every where by the Government of which this is the mother tongue. We need not contribute for its development; nor can you do anything more worthwhile than the Government for it. Of course, Sanskrit, our own language which is not supported by anyone today, needs your help . . . You should allot teaching hours like this: out of 6 hours, give 3 hours for Sanskrit, 2 for English and 1 for Urdu and Persian.[32]

Letter from Dayānanda to Mulraj, 12 March 1882

A conference is taking place at the moment . . . in Calcutta for deciding the medium of instruction in the schools. A memorial bearing the signatures of thousands of men should be sent in favour of Sanskrit and Hindi. Also send this information to Merut, Dehradun and other Samajas in the East.[33]

Acquisition of Knowledge

Both the teachers and their scholars should avoid all those things that act as hindrances in the way of the acquisition of knowledge, such as the company of wicked and lascivious people, contraction of bad habits (such as the use of intoxicants), fornication, child-marriage, want of perfect *Brahmacharya*, want of love on the part of the rulers, parents and learned men for the dissemination of knowledge of the *Veda* and other *Shastras*, over-eating, keeping late hours, sloth in learning, teaching, examining or being examined, or performing these duties with dishonesty, not regarding knowledge as the highest thing in the world . . . leaving off the worship of one true God, and wasting time in going about from place to place for the purpose of seeing and worshipping images made of stone, and other inanimate objects . . .[34]

It follows, therefore, that the teachers and students should possess excellent qualities. The teachers should so endeavour as to produce in their scholars such good qualities as truthfulness in word, deed and thought, culture, self-control, gentleness of disposition, perfect development of mind and body, so that they may become well-versed in the *Vedas* and *Shastras*. The teachers should always be diligent in eradicating evil habits of their scholars and in imparting knowledge. The scholars should always cultivate self-control, mental tranquillity, love for their tutors, thoughtfulness and habits of diligence. They should exert themselves as to acquire perfect knowledge, perfect *dharma*, perfect development of body (to enable them to live to the fullest age allotted to man), and learn to labour. Such are the duties of *Brahmans*.[35]

Diet

The use of all such foods and drinks as are obtained through injuring or killing others or through theft, dishonesty, breach of faith, fraud or hypocrisy is *forbidden*, in other words they all come under the heading of *forbidden* articles of diet; while the acquisition of foods and drinks through righteous means without injuring or killing any living creatures falls into the category of *permissible* articles, of diet.[36]

After some time of solitude at Rishikesh, a *bramachari* and two mountain ascetics joined me, and we all three went to Tehri.[37] The place was full of ascetics and *rajya-panditas* (royal priests). One of them invited me to come and have dinner with him at his house. At the appointed hour he sent a man to conduct me safely to his place, and both the *brahmachari* and myself followed the messenger. But to our dismay we saw upon entering the house a Brahmana preparing and cutting meat. Proceeding further into the interior apartment, we found a large number of *pandits* seated with a pyramid of flesh, rumpsteaks, and dressed-up heads of animals before them. The master of the house cordially invited me in, but, with a few brief words begging them to proceed with their good work and not to disturb themselves on my account, I left the house and returned to my own quarters. A few minutes later, the meat-eating *pandita* was at my side, praying me to return, and trying to excuse himself by saying that it was on my account that the sumptuous viands had been prepared. I told him that it was all useless; they were carnivorous, flesh-eating men and myself a strict vegetarian, who felt sick at the very sight of meat. If he insisted on providing me with food he might send me a few provisions of grain and vegetables which my *bramachari* would prepare for me. This he promised to do, and then, very much confused, he retired.[38]

Ārya Samāj

The principles of the Ārya Samāj enunciated at Bombay in 1875 and finally settled at Lahore in 1877 were:

1. Of all true knowledge and whatever is known from knowledge, the primary cause is God.
2. God is an embodiment of truth, intelligence and bliss, and one without form, all powerful, just, kind, unborn, infinite, unchangeable, beginningless, incomparable, supporter of all, lord of all, all-pervading, omniscient, undeteriorable, immortal, fearless, eternal, holy and creator of the universe. He alone is worthy of worship.
3. The *Vedas* are the books of all true knowledge. It is the paramount duty of all Aryas to read them, to teach them, to hear them and to preach them.
4. We should be ever ready to accept truth and renounce untruth.
5. Everything should be done according to *dharma*, i.e., after considering what is truth and what is untruth.

6. The chief object of the Arya Samaj is to do good to the world, i.e., to make physical, spiritual and social improvement.
7. We should treat all with love, and justice according to their deserts.
8. We should dispel ignorance and diffuse knowledge.
9. Nobody should remain contented with his personal progress. One should count the progress of all as one's own.
10. Everyone should consider oneself as bound in obeying social and all benefiting rules, but everyone is free in matters pertaining to individual well-being.[39]

Hence if you are anxious for the advancement of your country, you would do well to join the *Arya Samaj* and conduct yourself in accordance with its aims and objects. Otherwise, you (will simply waste your lives) and gain nothing in the end. It behoves us all to lovingly devote ourselves with all our heart, with all our wealth, and aye even with our lives, to the good of our country, the land of our birth, the land of the products of which we have lived, the land which sustains us still and will continue to do so in the future. No other *Samaj* or Society can equal the *Arya Samaj* in its power to raise *Aryavarta*. It will be a very good thing, indeed, if you would all help this *Samaj*, as the capability of a *Samaj* or Society to do good depends not on any single individual, but on all the members that support it.[40]

NOTES

1   *Satyarth Prakash*, (New Delhi, 1975), 723.
2   Ibid., iii – iv.
3   Ibid., 75.
4   Ibid., 725 – 6.
5   Ibid., 237.
6   *Autobiography of Dayananda Sarasvati*, (New Delhi, 1978), 69.
7   Ibid., 25 – 6.
8   *Satyarth Prakash*, 372 – 3.
9   Ibid., 383 – 4.
10 Ibid., 397.
11 Ibid., 725.
12 Ibid., 203.
13 Ibid., 219.
14 Ibid., 373.
15 Ibid., 233.
16 *Autobiography*, 83 – 4.
17 *Satyarth Prakash*, 247.

18   *Autobiography*, 84.
19   *Satyarth Prakash*, 310.
20   Ibid., 287.
21   *Autobiography*, 85.
22   *Satyarth Prakash*, 334 – 5.
23   Ibid., 103.
24   Ibid., 79 – 80.
25   Ibid., 110.
26   Ibid., 90.
27   Ibid., 94.
28   Ibid., 129.
29   *Autobiography*, 88.
30   *Satyarth Prakash*, 131.
31   *Autobiography*, 65.
32   Ibid., 70.
33   Ibid., 71.
34   *Satyarth Prakash*, 76.
35   Ibid., 127 – 8.
36   Ibid., 323.
37   Tehri: a sacred place on the Ganges about 14 miles above Hardwar.
38   *Autobiography*, 36.
39   Ibid., 55 – 6.
40   *Satyarth Prakash*, 475.

REFERENCES

Autobiography of Dayananda Sarasvati. Edited by K.C. Yadav. Second Revised
   Edition. New Delhi: Manohar Publications, 1978.
Light of Truth or An English Translation of the Satyarth Prakash. Dr Chiranjiva
   Bharadwaja. New Delhi: Sarvadeshik Arya Pratinidhi Sabha, 1975.

5

RĀMAKRISHNA (1836 – 1886)

Rāmakrishna was undoubtedly one of the most remarkable religious leaders of his time. Born in the Bengal village of Kamarpukur, which today houses a temple dedicated to him, he was involved from his early days in the religious festivals of the region. At the age of six or seven he is reputed to have experienced a mystical trance, an experience that was to occur many times subsequently during his life. Though lacking formal education because of inadequate schooling he possessed an abundance of native intelligence and welcomed the opportunity to join his brother Ramkumar at the Sanskrit school in Calcutta and later with the help of a wealthy lady named Rani Rasmani at the Kālī temple at Dakshineswar. It was here from 1856 that he remained for the rest of his life as a Brahmin priest devoted to the worship of the goddess Kālī.

He submitted himself to strenuous spiritual discipline for over a decade in an attempt to experience communion with God and was rewarded with mystical visions of the Divine as Kālī, Sītā, Rāma and Krishna. Through his associations with Bhairavi, a female ascetic of the Tantric school, he received instruction in yogic techniques which enabled him to control his spiritual energy. Later, through contact with two itinerant monks Jatadhari, a Vaiṣṇavite, and Tota Puri, a Advaitin, he deepened his understanding of the ways of bhakti and jñāna as means of union with the Divine. He learned also the distinction between savikalpa and nirvikalpa samadhi. In 1866 he was introduced by Govinda Roy to the worship of Allah and later became acquainted with Christian devotional practices. He was moved by a picture of the Madonna and child to experience visions of Christ and became so filled with the love of Christ as to be convinced of the incarnational status of Jesus.

From his personal experience of different religions he was able to claim that they were simply different paths to the same goal even as rivers flowed into the same ocean. Kālī the Divine Mother, and Brahman were two aspects of the same reality. Similarly the mystical experience of Christ in his view was at one with the mystical experience of Allah. All religions are true: God may be called by different names but he is one not many even as water may be given different names but is the same substance. It follows that it is not necessary to make a choice between the formless Absolute and the personal God: the difference between them is no more than that between ice and water.

The impediments to spiritual development, according to Rāmakrishna, are 'woman' and 'gold', that is, worldliness in the form of lust and greed. Lust is overcome when all women are regarded as embodiments of the Divine Mother and greed is conquered when worldly interests and possessions are transcended. Worldliness is māyā and it is man's ignorance of his true Self which causes him to become enmeshed in māyā in the first place and deluded by 'woman' and 'gold'. Release is attained through that discrimination which recognizes God alone as real and eternal.

Rāmakrishna's emphasis on spiritual development may have been responsible for his critical attitude towards man's preoccupation with social reform. The danger of excessive reforming zeal was lack of altruism and the development of pride. Good works should not detract from devotion and should always be performed in the spirit of detachment. Social amelioration, including the removal of caste distinctions, should be the natural consequence of the love and worship of God.

Rāmakrishna's teaching attracted a dedicated group of disciples of whom Vivekānanda was the most prominent. They remained with him throughout his life and were responsible for disseminating knowledge of his teaching throughout India.

RĀMAKRISHNA

Religion

God can be realised through all paths. All religions are true. The important thing is to reach the roof. You can reach it by stone stairs or by wooden stairs or by bamboo steps or by a rope. You can also climb up by a bamboo pole . . .

You may say that there are many errors and superstitions in another religion. I should reply: Suppose there are. Every religion has errors. Everyone thinks that his watch gives the correct time. It is enough to have yearning for God. It is enough to love Him and feel attracted to Him.[1]

It is not good to feel that one's religion alone is true and all others are false. God is one only and not two. Different people call him by different names: some as Allah, some as God, and others as Krishna, Siva, and Brahman. It is like water in a lake. Some drink it at one place and call it 'jal', others at another place and call it 'pani', and still others at a third place and call it 'water'. The Hindus call it 'jal', the Christians 'water', and the Mussulmans 'pani'. But it is one and the same thing. Opinions are but paths. Each religion is only a path leading to God, as rivers come from different directions and ultimately become one in the one ocean.

All religions and all paths call upon their followers to pray to one and the same God. Therefore one should not show disrespect to any religion or religious opinion.[2]

The Eternal Religion, the religion of the rishis, has been in existence from time out of mind and will exist eternally. There exist in this Sanatana Dharma all forms of worship — worship of God with form and worship of the Impersonal Deity as well. It contains all paths — the path of knowledge, the path of devotion, and so on. Other forms of religion, the modern cults, will remain for a few days and then disappear.[3]

God, Brahman, Kālī

But the Reality is one and the same. The difference is only in name. He who is Brahman is verily Atman, and again, He is the Bhagavan. He is Brahman to the followers of the path of knowledge, Paramatman to the yogis, and Bhagavan to the lovers of God.[4]

The Primordial Power is ever at play. She is creating, preserving, and destroying in play as it were. This power is called Kali. Kali is verily Brahman, and Brahman is verily Kali. It is one and the same Reality. When we think of It as inactive, that is to say, not engaged in the acts of creation, preservation and destruction, then we call it Brahman. But when It engages in these activities, then we call It Kali or Sakti. The reality is one and the same; the difference is in name and form.[5]

Is Kali, my Divine Mother, of a black complexion? She appears black because She is viewed from a distance, but when intimately known She is no longer so.[6]

Think of Brahman, Existence-Knowledge-Bliss Absolute, as a shoreless ocean. Through the cooling influence, as it were, of the bhakta's love, the water has frozen at places into blocks of ice. In other words, God now and then assumes various forms for His lovers and reveals Himself to them as a Person. But with the rising of the sun of Knowledge, the blocks of ice melt. Then one doesn't feel any more that God is a Person, nor does one see God's forms.[7]

Existence-Knowledge-Bliss Absolute is one, and one only. But It is associated with different limiting adjuncts on account of the different degrees of Its manifestation. That is why one finds various forms of God. The devotee sings, 'O my Divine Mother, Thou are all these!' Wherever you see actions, like creation, preservation, and dissolution, there is the manifestation of Sakti.[8]

God dwells in all beings. But you may be intimate only with good people; you must keep away from the evil-minded. God is even in the tiger; but you cannot embrace a tiger on that account. (Laughter.) You may say 'Why run away from a tiger, which is also a manifestation of God?' The answer to that is: 'Those who tell you to run away are also manifestations of God — and why shouldn't you listen to them?'[9]

Do you know what God with form is like? Like bubbles rising on an expanse of water, various divine forms are seen to rise out of the Great Akasa of Consciousness. The Incarnation of God is one of these forms. The Primal Energy sports as it were, through the activities of a Divine Incarnation.[10]

God has different forms, and He sports in different ways. He sports as Isvara, deva, man, and the universe. In every age he descends to earth in human form, as an Incarnation, to teach people love and devotion.[11]

The inferior devotee says, 'God exists, but He is very far off, up there in heaven.' The mediocre devotee says, 'God exists in all beings as life and consciousness.' The superior devotee says: 'It is God Himself who has become everything; whatever I see is only a form of God. It is He alone who has become maya, the universe, and all living beings. Nothing exists but God.'[12]

God with form is as real as God without form. Do you know what describing God as being only formless is like? It is like a man's playing only a monotone on his flute, though it has seven holes. But on the same instrument another man plays different melodies. Likewise, in how many ways the believers in a Personal God enjoy Him! They enjoy Him through many different attitudes: the serene attitude, the attitude of a servant, a friend, a mother, a husband, or a lover.[13]

Men often think they have understood Brahman fully. Once an ant went to a hill of sugar. One grain filled its stomach. Taking another grain in its mouth it started homeward. On its way it thought, 'Next time I shall carry home the whole hill.' That is the way shallow minds think. They don't know that Brahman is beyond one's words and thought. However great a man may be, how much can he know of Brahman? Sukadeva and sages like him may have been big ants; but even they could carry at the utmost eight or ten grains of sugar![14]

The Divine Mother

My Divine Mother is not only formless, She has forms as well. One can see Her forms. One can behold Her incomparable beauty through feeling and love. The Mother reveals Herself to Her devotees in different forms.[15]

Govinda: Reverend sir, why does the Divine Mother have a black complexion?

Master: You see Her as black because you are far away from Her. Go near and you will find Her devoid of all colour. The water of a lake appears black from a distance. Go near and take the water in your hand, and you will see that it has no colour at all. Similarly, the sky looks blue from a distance. But look at the atmosphere near you; it has no colour. The nearer you come to

God, the more you will realise that He has neither name nor form.[16]

The Divine Mother revealed to me in the Kali Temple[17] that it was She who had become everything. She showed me that everything was full of Consciousness. The Image was Consciousness, the altar was Consciousness, the water-vessels were Consciousness, the door-sill was Consciousness, the marble floor was Consciousness — all was Consciousness.[18]

God has created the world at play, as it were. This is called Mahamaya, the Great Illusion. Therefore one must take a refuge in the Divine Mother, the Cosmic Power Itself. It is She who has bound us with the shackles of illusion. The realisation of God is possible only when those shackles are severed . . .

One must propitiate the Divine Mother, the Primal Energy, in order to obtain God's grace.[19]

Duties

People who carry to excess the giving of alms, or the distributing of food among the poor, fall victims to the desire of acquiring name and fame.

Sambhu Mallick once talked about establishing hospitals, dispensaries, and schools, making roads, digging public reservoirs, and so forth. I said to him: 'Don't go out of your way to look for such works. Undertake only those works that present themselves to you and are of pressing necessity — and those also in a spirit of detachment.' It is not good to become involved in many activities. That makes one forget God. Coming to the Kalighat Temple, some, perhaps spend their whole time in giving alms to the poor. They have no time to see the Mother in the inner shrine! (Laughter.) First of all manage somehow to see the image of the Divine Mother, even by pushing through the crowd. Then you may or may not give alms, as you wish. You may give to the poor to your heart's content, if you feel that way. Work is only a means to the realisation of God. Therefore I said to Sambhu, 'Suppose God appears before you; then, will you ask Him to build hospitals and dispensaries for you?' (Laughter.) A lover of God never says that. He will rather say: 'O Lord, give me a place at the Lotus Feet. Keep me always in Thy company. Give me sincere and pure love for Thee'.[20]

It is by no means necessary for a man always to be engaged in his duties. Actions drop away when one realises God, as the flower drops of itself when the fruit appears . . .

Live in the world as the mudfish lives in the mud. One develops love of God by going away from the world into solitude, now and then, and meditating on God. After that one can live in the world unattached. The mud is there, and the fish has to live in it, but his body is not stained by mud. Such a man can lead the life of a householder in a spirit of detachment.[21]

Lust is like the root of the tree, and desires are branches and twigs. One cannot completely get rid of the six passions: lust, anger, greed, and the like. Therefore one should direct them to God. If you must have desire and greed, then you should desire love of God and be greedy to attain Him. If you must be conceited and egotistic, then feel conceited and egotistic thinking that you are the servant of God, the child of God.[22]

Do your duty to the world after knowing God. With one hand hold to the Lotus Feet of the Lord and with the other do your work.[23]

Ego

According to the Vedanta one has to know the real nature of one's own Self. But such knowledge is impossible without the renunciation of ego. The ego is like a stick that seems to divide the water in two. It makes you feel that you are one and I am another. When the ego disappears in samadhi, then one knows Brahman to be one's own inner consciousness.[24]

'I' and 'mine' indicate ignorance. Without ignorance one cannot have such a feeling as 'I am the doer; these are my wife, children, possessions, name and fame' . . . The 'unripe I' makes one feel: 'I am the doer. These are my wife and children. I am a teacher.' Renounce this 'unripe I' and keep the 'ripe I', which will make you feel that you are the servant of God, His devotee, and that God is the Doer and you are His instrument.[25]

The 'I' that makes one a worldly person and attaches one to 'woman' and 'gold' is the 'wicked I'. The intervention of this ego creates the difference between jiva and Atman. Water appears to be divided into two parts if one puts a stick across it. But in reality there is only one water. It appears as two on account of the stick.

This 'I' is the stick. Remove the stick and there remains only one water as before.[26]

Even after attaining samadhi, some retain the 'servant ego' or the 'devotee ego'. The bhakta keeps this 'I-consciousness'. He says, 'O God, Thou art the Master and I am Thy servant; Thou art the Lord and I am thy devotee'. He feels that way even after the realization of God. His 'I' is not completely effaced.[27]

If one analyses oneself, one doesn't find any such thing as 'I'. Take an onion, for instance. First of all you peel off the red outer skin; then you find thick white skins. Peel these one after the other, and you won't find anything inside.

In that state a man no longer finds the existence of his ego. And who is there left to seek it? Who can describe how he feels in that state — in his own Pure Consciousness — about the real nature of Brahman? Once a salt doll went to measure the depth of the ocean. No sooner was it in the water than it dissolved. Now who was to tell the depth?

There is a sign of Perfect Knowledge. Man becomes silent when It is attained. Then the 'I', which may be likened to the salt doll, dissolves in the ocean of Existence-Knowledge-Bliss Absolute and becomes one with It. Not the slightest trace of distinction is left.[28]

Jñāna, Bhakti

The jnani experiences God-consciousness within himself; it is like the upper Ganges, flowing in only one direction. To him the whole universe is illusory, like a dream; he is always established in the Reality of Self. But with the lover of God the case is different. His feeling does not flow in only one direction. He feels both the ebb-tide and the flood-tide of divine emotion. He laughs and weeps and dances and sings in the ecstasy of God. The lover of God likes to sport with Him. In the Ocean of God-consciousness he sometimes swims, sometimes goes down, and sometimes rises to the surface — like pieces of ice in the water. (Laughter.)

The jnani seeks to realise Brahman. But the ideal of the Bhakta is the Personal God — a God endowed with omnipotence and with the six treasures.[29]

The best path for this age is bhaktiyoga, the path of bhakti prescribed by Narada:[30] to sing the name and glories of God and pray to Him with a longing Heart, 'O God, give me knowledge, give me devotion, and reveal Thyself to me!' The path of karma is extremely difficult.[31]

The path of knowledge is very difficult. One cannot obtain Knowledge unless one gets rid of the feeling that one is the body. In the Kaliyuga[32] the life of man is centred on food. He cannot get rid of the feeling that he is the body and the ego. Therefore the path of devotion is prescribed for this cycle. This is an easy path.[33]

It is not possible to develop ecstatic love of God unless you love Him very deeply and regard Him as your very own.

Listen to a story. Once three friends were going through a forest, when a tiger suddenly appeared before them. 'Brothers', one of them exclaimed, 'We are lost!' 'Why should you say that?', said the second friend. 'Why should we be lost? Come, let us pray to God.' The third friend said: 'No. Why should we trouble God about it? Come, let us climb this tree.'

The friend who said, 'We are lost!' did not know that there is a God who is our Protector. The friend who asked the others to pray to God was a jnani. He was aware that God is the Creator, Preserver, and Destroyer of the world. The third friend, who didn't want to trouble God with prayers and suggested climbing the tree, had ecstatic love of God. It is the very nature of such love that it makes a man think himself stronger than his Beloved. He is always alert lest his Beloved should suffer. The one desire of his life is to keep his Beloved from even being pricked in the foot by a thorn.[34]

World, Māyā

Maya is nothing but 'woman' and 'gold'. A man attains yoga when he has forced his mind from these two. The Self — the Supreme Self — is the magnet; the individual self is the needle. The individual self experiences the state of yoga when it is attracted by the Supreme Self to Itself. But the magnet cannot attract the needle if the needle is covered with clay; it can draw the needle only when the clay is removed. The clay of 'woman' and 'gold' must be removed.[35]

Neighbour: Then why should one call the world maya?

Master: As long as one has not realised God, one should renounce the world, following the process of 'Neti, neti'. But he who has attained God knows that it is God who has become all this. Then he sees that God, maya, living beings, and the universe form one whole. God includes the universe and its living beings.[36]

Vaikuntha: Is the world unreal?

Master: Yes, it is unreal as long as one has not realised God.

Through ignorance man forgets God and speaks always of 'I' and 'mine'. He sinks down and down, entangled in maya, deluded by 'woman' and 'gold'. Maya robs him of his knowledge of such an extent that he cannot find the way of escape, though such a way exists.[37]

Discrimination is the reasoning by which one knows that God alone is real and all else is unreal. Real means eternal, and unreal means impermanent. He who has acquired discrimination knows that God is the only Substance and all else is non-existent. With the awakening of this spirit of discrimination a man wants to know God. On the contrary, if a man loves the unreal — such things as creature comforts, name, fame, and wealth — then he doesn't want to know God, who is the very nature of Reality. Through discrimination between the Real and the unreal, one seeks to know God.[38]

God alone is the Real, that is to say, the Eternal Substance, and the world is unreal, that is to say, transitory. As soon as a man finds his mind wandering away to the unreal, he should apply discrimination. The moment an elephant stretches out its trunk to eat a plaintain-tree in a neighbour's garden, it gets a blow from the iron goad of the driver.[39]

God alone is Substance, and all else illusory. God alone is real, and all else has only a two-days' existence. What is there in the world? The world is like a pickled hog plum: one craves for it. But what is there in a hog plum? Only skin and pith. And if you eat it you will have colic.[40]

Wealth

Once a rich man came here and said to me: 'Sir, you must do something so that I may win my lawsuit. I have heard of your reputation and so I have come here.' 'My dear sir', I said to him, 'you have made a mistake. I am not the person you are looking for; Achalananda is your man.'

A true devotee of God does not care for such things as wealth or health. He thinks: 'Why should I practise spiritual austerities for creative comforts, money, or name and fame? These are all impermanent. They last only a day or two.'[41]

Caste

The caste system can be removed by one means only, and that is the love of God. Lovers of God do not belong to any caste. The mind, body, and soul of a man become purified through divine love. Chaitanya and Nityananda scattered the name of Hari to everyone, including the pariah, and embraced them all. A brahmin without this love is no longer a brahmin. And the pariah with the love of God is no longer a pariah. Through bhakti an untouchable becomes pure and elevated.[42]

Women

One may regard woman as one's mistress or look on oneself as her handmaid or as her child. I look on woman as my mother. To look on oneself as her handmaid is also good; but it is extremely difficult to practise spiritual discipline looking on woman as one's mistress. To regard oneself as her child is a very pure attitude.[43]

I worshipped the 'Beautiful' in a girl fourteen years old. I saw that she was the personification of the Divine Mother. At the end of the worship I bowed down before her and offered a rupee at her feet. One day I witnessed a Ramlila performance. I saw the performers to be the actual Sita, Rama, Lakshmana, Hanuman, and Vibhishana. Then I worshipped the actors and actresses who played those parts.

At that time I used to invite maidens here and worship them. I found them to be embodiments of the Divine Mother Herself.

One day I saw a women in blue standing near the bakul-tree. She was a prostitute. But she instantly kindled in me the vision of Sita.[44]

All women are the embodiments of Sakti. It is the Primal Power that has become women and appears to us in the form of women.[45]

He is a holy man who does not regard women with the eyes of a worldly person. He never forgets to look upon a woman as his mother, and to offer her his worship if he happens to be near her.[46]

Four classes of men

Men may be divided into four classes: those bound by the fetters of the world, the seekers after liberation, the liberated, and the ever-free.

Among the ever-free we may count sages like Narada. They live in the world for the good of others, to teach men spiritual truth.

Those in bondage are sunk in worldliness and forgetful of God. Not even by mistake do they think of God.

The seekers after liberation want to free themselves from attachment to the world. Some of them succeed and others do not.

The liberated souls, such as the sadhus and mahatmas, are not entangled in the world, in 'women and gold'. Their minds are free from worldliness. Besides, they always meditate on the Lotus Feet of God.

Suppose a net has been cast into a lake to catch fish. Some fish are so clever that they are never caught in the net. They are like the ever-free. But most of the fish are entangled in the net. Some of them try to free themselves from it, and they are like those who seek liberation. But not all the fish that struggle succeed. A very few do jump out of the net, making a big splash in the water. Then the fishermen shout, 'Look! There goes a big one!' But most of the fish caught in the net cannot escape, nor do they make any effort to get out. On the contrary, they burrow into the mud with the net in their mouths and lie there quietly, thinking, 'We need not fear any more; we are quite safe here.' But the poor things do not know that the fisherman will drag them out with the net. These are like men bound to the world.[47]

Rebirth

The potter puts his pots in the sun to dry. Haven't you noticed that among them there are both baked and unbaked ones? When a cow happens to walk over them, some of the pots get broken to pieces. The broken parts that are already baked, the potter throws away, since they are of no more use to him. But the soft ones, though broken, he gathers up. He makes them into a lump and out of this forms new pots. In the same way, so long as a man has not realised God, he will have to come back again to the Potter's hand, that is, he will have to be born again and again.[48]

NOTES

1   *The Gospel of Sri Ramakrishna*, (Madras, 1969), 39.
2   Ibid., 204, 249.
3   Ibid., 356.
4   Ibid., 63.
5   Ibid., 64.
6   Ibid., 65.
7   Ibid., 78.
8   Ibid., 218.
9   Ibid., 8.
10   Ibid., 113.
11   Ibid., 196.
12   Ibid., 205.
13   Ibid., 152.
14   Ibid., 28 – 9.
15   Ibid., 108.
16   Ibid., 211.
17   Located at Dakshineswar.
18   *Gospel*, 290.
19   Ibid., 43.
20   Ibid., 72.
21   Ibid., 280.
22   Ibid., 379 – 80.
23   Ibid., 269.
24   Ibid., 336.
25   Ibid., 209.
26   Ibid., 102 – 3.
27   Ibid., 104.
28   Ibid., 78 – 9.
29   Ibid., 217.
30   Narada: great sage of Hindu mythology.
31   *Gospel*, 406.
32   Kaliyuga: fourth and present world-cycle characterized by excess of vice and lack of virtue.
33   *Gospel*, 103.
34   Ibid., 165 – 6.
35   Ibid., 288.
36   Ibid., 271.
37   Ibid., 268.
38   Ibid., 271.
39   Ibid., 22.
40.   Ibid., 903.
41   Ibid., 227.
42   Ibid., 85 – 6.
43   Ibid., 51.
44   Ibid., 168.
45   Ibid., 218.
46   Ibid., 270.
47   Ibid., 11.
48   Ibid., 367.

REFERENCE

The Gospel of Sri Ramakrishna. Originally recorded in Bengali by M. (Mahendranath Gupta). Translated by Swami Nikhilananda. Madras: Sri Ramakrishna Math, Mylapore, 1969.

6

VIVEKĀNANDA (1863 – 1902)

Referred to by delegates at the Parliament of Religions meeting in
Chicago in 1893 as the 'cyclonic monk from India' Narendranāth
Datta, better known as Vivekānanda, was born into an
aristocratic family in Calcutta. As a college student he was
renowned for his oratory and debating powers but he also
displayed a meditative tendency that kept him aloof from his
fellow students. He was inclined to rationalism and was impressed
both by the analytic approach of Western science and the writings
of the leaders of the Brahmo Samāj. His rational and analytic
outlook suffered a change, however, when he met Rāmakrishna in 1881 and his intention to embark on a legal career was
set aside. After an initial period of questioning he surrendered to
Rāmakrishna's influence and became his foremost disciple taking
the name of Vivekānanda.

In pursuit of his spiritual mission he travelled the length and
breadth of India visiting all the important centres of learning,
acquainting himself with the diverse religious traditions of the
country and the many different patterns of social life. He
developed a sympathy for the suffering and poverty of the under-
privileged and resolved to arouse the nation from its lethargy and
inertia. The divinity of man became a significant tenet in his
teaching and he saw the service of the poor and deprived as
synonymous with the service of God.

The Vedāntic doctrine of the divinity of man was one aspect of
the message Vivekānanda proclaimed at the World Parliament of
Religions in Chicago. It meant, as he tried to show, that India's
greatest need in view of her hungry masses was not missionaries
bent on conversion or the erection of Christian churches, but
bread to save the people from starvation. Another aspect of his
message was the essential unity of all religions which was not
inconsistent with the preservation of diversity. What should be
aimed for, he claimed, was not the elimination of different
religions but the mutual recognition of the value of different
traditions and a readiness to assimilate the spirit of one another.

From his four years sojourn in the West Vivekānanda came to
recognize the significant contribution Western science and technology could make to man's material well-being, but he was

equally convinced that to progress spiritually Western man would need to look to the East. His ideal was that India should conquer the world with her spirituality. Hence his unfailing efforts on his return to India to arouse his fellow countrymen to the potency of their spiritual heritage. He toured India with his message that spirituality was the basis of Hindu civilization and the fountainhead of social reform. He founded the Rāmakrishna Mission at Belur near Calcutta in 1897 to train men to teach Vedāntic ideals and to serve their fellow men without regard for caste distinctions. Emphasis was placed on alleviating suffering, child welfare, education and charitable works, and great importance was attached to spiritual dedication.

He regarded the provision of education for the Indian people as a primary duty. It was essential for the uplift of the lower classes, the restoration of their humanity and the development of their individuality. Given education they could work out their own salvation, and the aid of self-sacrificing sannyāsins could be elicited to provide them with this service as they travelled from one village to another. His ambition was to institute a programme of education that would enable all Hindus, whatever their status in society, to determine their own destiny, yet he recognized that caste was the greatest divisive factor in Hinduism and a form of bondage.

Vivekānanda's stress on the divinity of man meant that he saw God in every man. The difference between one man and another, in his view, was a difference of degree and not of kind. The same applied to the universe as a whole since God permeates all that exists from plants and stones to human beings. So to maintain that animals were created by God in order to provide man with food would be contrary to Vedāntic teaching and to belief in the fundamental unity of all existence.

Vivekānanda's enthusiasm in the pursuance of his spiritual mission and social reforms meant that he eventually burnt himself out in the cause of his fellow countrymen, but not before he had inculcated in them a sense of pride in the cultural heritage of Hinduism and established himself as one of the great leaders and reformers of his generation.

VIVEKĀNANDA (NARENDRANĀTH DATTA)

Religion

By the study of different religions we find that in essence they are one. When I was a boy, this scepticism reached me, and it seemed for a time as if I must give up all hope of religion. But fortunately for me I studied the Christian religion, the Mohammedan, the Buddhistic, and others, and what was my surprise to find that the same foundation principles taught by my religion were also taught by all religions . . . We see, therefore, that if one religion is true, all others must be true. There are differences in non-essentials, but in essentials they are all one.[1]

Get rid, in the first place, of all these limited ideas and see God in every person — working through all hands, walking through all feet, and eating through every mouth. In every being He lives, through all minds He thinks. He is self-evident, nearer unto us than ourselves. To know this is religion, is faith, and may it please the Lord to give us this faith! When we shall feel that oneness, we shall be immortal. We are physically immortal even, one with the universe. So long as there is one that breathes throughout the universe, I live in that one. I am not this limited little being, I am the universal.[2]

The difference between man and man, between angels and man, between man and animals, between animals and plants, between plants and stones is not in kind, because everyone from the highest angel to the lowest particle of matter is but an expression of that one infinite ocean, and the difference is only in degree. I am a low manifestation, you may be a higher, but in both the materials are the same. You and I are both outlets of the same channel, and that is God; as such, your nature is God, and so is mine . . . The sum-total of this whole universe is God Himself.[3]

One principle it (Vedanta) lays down — and that, the Vedanta claims, is to be found in every religion in the world — that man is divine, that all this which we see around us is the outcome of the consciousness of the divine. Everything that is strong, and good, and powerful in human nature is the outcome of that divinity, and though potential in many, there is no difference between man and man essentially, all being alike divine. There is, as it were, an infinite ocean behind, and you and I are so many waves, coming out of that infinite ocean; and each one of us is trying his best to manifest that infinite outside. So, potentially, each one of us has that infinite ocean of Existence, Knowledge, and Bliss as our birthright, our real nature; and the difference between us is caused by the greater or lesser power to manifest that divine. Therefore the Vedanta lays down that each man should be treated not as what he manifests, but as what he stands for.[4]

There is but one life, one world, one existence. Everything is that One, the difference is in degree and not in kind. The difference between our lives is not in kind. The Vedanta entirely denies such ideas as that animals are separate from men, and that they were made and created by God to be used for our food.[5]

Are all the religions of the world really contradictory? I do not mean the external forms in which great thoughts are clad. I do not mean the different buildings, languages, rituals, books, etc. employed in various religions, but I mean the internal soul of every religion. Every religion has a soul behind it, and that soul may differ from the soul of another religion; but are they contradictory? . . . I believe that they are not contradictory; they are supplementary. Each religion, as it were, takes up one part of the great universal truth, and spends its whole force in embodying and typifying that part of the great truth. It is, therefore, addition, not exclusion. That is the idea.[6]

What then do I mean by the ideal of a universal religion? I do not mean any one universal philosophy, or any one universal mythology, or any one universal ritual held alike by all; for I know that this world must go on working wheel within wheel, this intricate mass of machinery, most complex, most wonderful. What can *we* do then? We can make it run smoothly, we can lessen the friction, we can grease the wheels, as it were. How? By recognising the natural necessity of variation. Just as we have recognised unity by our very nature, so we must also recognise variation. We must learn that truth may be expressed in a hundred thousand ways, and that each of these ways is true as far as it goes.[7]

You hear claims made by every religion as being the universal religion of the world. Let me tell you in the first place that perhaps there never will be such a thing, but if there is a religion which can lay claim to be that, it is only our religion and no other, because every other religion depends on some person or persons. All the other religions have been built round the life of what they think a historical man; and what they think the strength of religion is really the weakness, for disprove the historicity of the man and the whole fabric tumbles to the ground. Half the lives of these great founders of religions have been broken into pieces, and the other half doubted very seriously. As such every truth that had its sanction only in their words vanishes into air. But the truths of our religion, although we have persons by the score, do not depend on them.[8]

Religion is the manifestation of the Divinity already in man.[9]

I propound a philosophy which can serve as a basis to every possible religious system in the world, and my attitude towards all of them is one of extreme sympathy — my teaching is antagonistic to none. I direct my attention to the individual, to make him strong, to teach him that he himself is divine, and I call upon men to make themselves conscious of this divinity within. That is really the ideal — conscious or unconscious — of every religion.[10]

People of the West should learn one thing from India and that is toleration. All the religions are good, since the essentials are the same.[11]

It is a most glorious dispensation of the Lord that there are so many religions in the world; and would to God that these would increase every day, until every man had a religion unto himself!

Vedanta understands that and therefore preaches the one principle and admits various methods. It has nothing to say against anyone — whether you are a Christian, or a Buddhist, or a Jew, or a Hindu, whatever mythology you believe, whether you owe allegiance to the prophet of Nazareth, or of Mecca, or of India, or of anywhere else, whether you yourself are a prophet — it has nothing to say. It only preaches the principle which is the background of every religion and of which all the prophets and saints and seers are but illustrations and manifestations.[12]

No one form of religion will do for all. Each is a pearl on a string. We must be particular above all else to find individuality in each. No man is born to any religion; he has a religion in his soul. Any system which seeks to destroy individuality is in the long run disastrous. Each life has a current running through it, and this current will eventually take it to God. The end and aim of all religions is to realise God. The greatest of all training is to worship God alone. If each man chose his own ideal and stuck to it, all religious controversy would vanish.[13]

The greatest name man ever gave to God is Truth. Truth is the fruit of realisation; therefore seek it within the soul. Get away

from all books and forms and let your soul see its Self . . .
Religion is one, but its application must be various. Let each one,
therefore, give his message; but not find the defects in other religions. You must come out from all form if you would see the
Light. Drink deep of the nectar of knowledge of God. The man
who realises, 'I am He', though clad in rags, is happy. Go forth
into the Eternal and come back with eternal energy. The slave
goes out to search for Truth; he comes back free.[14]

This is the last word of the Vedas. It begins with dualism, goes
through a qualified monism and ends in perfect monism. We
know how very few in this world can come to the last, or even
dare to believe in it, and fewer still dare act according to it. Yet we
know that therein lies the explanation of all ethics, of all morality
and all spirituality in the universe . . .

Now as society exists at the present time, all these three stages
are necessary; the one does not deny the other, one is simply the
fulfilment of the other. The Advaitist or the qualified Advaitist
does not say the dualism is wrong; it is a right view, but a lower
one. It is on the way to truth; therefore let everyone work out his
own vision of this universe, according to his own ideas.[15]

God

What is the outcome of the philosophy? It is that the idea of a
Personal God is not sufficient. We have to get to something
higher, to the Impersonal idea. It is the only logical step that we
can take. Not that the personal idea would be destroyed by that,
not that we supply proof that the Personal God does not exist, but
we must go to the Impersonal for the explanation of the personal,
for the Impersonal is a much higher generalisation than the personal. The Impersonal only can be Infinite, the personal is
limited.[16]

My idea is that what you call a Personal God is the same as the
Impersonal Being, a Personal and Impersonal God at the same
time. We are personalised impersonal beings. If you use the word
in the abolute sense, we are impersonal; but if you use it in a
relative meaning, we are personal . . . When we talk of God
speaking, we say He speaks through His universe; and when we
speak of Him beyond all limitations of time and space, we say He
is an Impersonal Being. Yet He is the same Being.[17]

God exists; but He is not the man sitting upon a cloud. He is
pure Spirit. Where does He reside? Nearer to you than your very

self. He is the Soul. How can you perceive God as separate and different from yourself? When you think of Him as some one separate from yourself, you do not know Him. He is you yourself. That was the doctrine of the prophets of India.[18]

Divinity in Man

My ideal indeed can be put in a few words and that is: to preach unto mankind their divinity, and how to make it manifest in every moment of life.[19]

Christs and Buddhas are simply occasions upon which to objectify our own inner powers. We really answer our own prayers.

It is blasphemy to think that if Jesus had never been born, humanity would not have been saved. It is horrible to forget thus the divinity in human nature, a divinity that must come out. Never forget the glory of human nature. We are the greatest God that ever was or ever will be. Christs and Buddhas are but waves on the boundless ocean which *I am*. Bow down to nothing but your own higher Self. Until you know that you are that very God of gods, there will never be any freedom for you.[20]

Do you not remember what the Bible says, 'If you cannot love your brother whom you have seen, how can you love God whom you have not seen?' If you cannot see God in the human face, how can you see him in the clouds, or in images made of dull, dead matter, or in mere fictitious stories of our brain? I shall call you religious from the day you begin to see God in men and women, and there you will understand what is meant by turning the left cheek to the man who strikes you on the right. When you see man as God, everything, even the tiger, will be welcome. Whatever comes to you is but the Lord, the Eternal, the Blessed One, appearing to us in various forms, as our father, and mother, and friend, and child — they are our own soul playing with us.[21]

Idolatry

It has become a trite saying that idolatry is wrong, and every man swallows it at the present time without questioning. I once thought so, and to pay the penalty of that I had to learn my lesson sitting at the feet of a man who realised everything through idols; I allude to Ramakrishna Paramahamsa. If such Ramakrishna Paramahansas are produced by idol-worship, what will you have — the reformer's creed or any number of idols? I want an answer.

Take a thousand idols more if you can produce Ramakrishna Paramahamsas through idol-worship, and may god speed you! Produce such noble natures by any means you can.[22]

Those reformers who preach against image-worship, or what they denounce as idolatry — to them I say, 'Brothers, if you are fit to worship God-without-form discarding all external help, do so, but why do you condemn others who cannot do the same?. . .'[23]

God in Everyone

Look upon every man, woman, and every one as God. You cannot help anyone, you can only serve: serve the children of the Lord, serve the Lord Himself, if you have the privilege. If the Lord grants that you can help any one of His children, blessed you are; do not think too much of yourselves. Blessed you are that that privilege was given to you when others had it not. Do it only as a worship. I should see God in the poor, and it is for my salvation that I go and worship them. The poor and the miserable are for our salvation, so that we may serve the Lord, coming in the shape of the diseases, coming in the shape of the lunatic, the leper, and the sinner! Bold are my words; and let me repeat that it is the greatest privilege in our life that we are allowed to serve the Lord in all these shapes.[24]

Social Reform

Caste

It is in the nature of society to form itself into groups; and what will go will be these privileges. Caste is a natural order; I can perform one duty in social life, and you another; you can govern a country, and I can mend a pair of old shoes, but that is no reason why you are greater than I, for can you mend shoes? Can I govern the country? I am clever in mending shoes, you are clever in reading Vedas, but that is no reason why you should trample on my head . . . Caste is good. That is the only natural way of solving life. Men must form themselves into groups, and you cannot get rid of that. Wherever you go, there will be caste. But that does not mean that there should be these privileges . . . And that is what we want, as privilege for any one, equal chances for all; let every one be taught that the divine is within, and everyone will work out his own salvation.[25]

The solution of the caste problem in India, therefore, assumes this form, not to degrade the higher castes, not to crush out the Brahmin. The Brahminhood is the ideal of humanity in India, as wonderfully put forward by Shankaracharya at the beginning of his commentary on the Gita, where he speaks about the reason for Krishna's coming as a preacher for the preservation of Brahminhood, of Brahminness. That was the great end. This Brahmin, the man of God, he who has known Brahman, the ideal man, the perfect man, must remain; He must not go. And with all the defects of the caste now, we know that we must all be ready to give to the Brahmins this credit, that from them have come more men with real Brahminness in them than from all the other castes. . .

The solution is not by bringing down the higher, but by raising the lower up to the level of the higher . . . The ideal at the one end is the Brahmin and the ideal at the other end is the Chandala, and the whole work is to raise the Chandala up to the Brahmin.[26]

I have received Kidi's letters. With the question whether castes shall go or come, I have nothing to do. My idea is to bring to the door of the meanest, the poorest, the noble ideas that the human race has developed both in and out of India, and let them think for themselves. Whether there should be caste or not, whether women should be perfectly free or not, does not concern me. 'Liberty of thought and action is the only condition of life, of growth and well-being.' Where it does not exist, the man, the race, the nation must go down.

Caste or no caste, creed or no creed, any man, or class, or caste, or nation, or institution which bars the power of free thought and action of an individual — even so long as that power does not injure others — is devilish and must go down.

My whole ambition in life is to set in motion a machinery which will bring noble ideas to the door of everybody, and then let men and women settle their own fate.[27]

Another great discrepancy: the conviction is daily gaining on my mind is the idea of caste is the greatest dividing factor and the root of Maya; all caste either on the principle of birth or of merit is bondage.[28]

Education

Therefore, even for social reform, the first duty is to educate the people, and you will have to wait till that time comes. Most of the reforms that have been agitated for during the past century have been ornamental. Every one of these reforms only touches the first two castes, and no other. The question of widow marriage would not touch seventy per cent of the Indian women, and all such questions only reach the higher castes of Indian people who are educated, mark you, at the expense of the masses. Every effort has been spent in cleaning their own houses. But that is no reformation. You must go down to the basis of the thing, to the very root of the matter. That is what I call radical reform. Put the fire there and let it burn upwards and make an Indian nation.[29]

The chief cause of India's ruin has been the monopolising of the whole education and intelligence of the land, by dint of pride and royal authority, among a handful of men. If we are to rise again, we shall have to do it in the same way, i.e. by spreading education among the masses.[30]

Education of Poor

The one thing that is at the root of all evils in India is the condition of the poor. The poor in the West are devils; compared to them ours are angels, and it is therefore so much easier to raise our poor. The only service to be done for our lower classes is to give them education, *to develop their lost individuality*. That is the great task between our people and princes. Up to now nothing has been done in that direction. Priest-power and foreign conquest have trodden them down for centuries, and at last the poor of India have forgotten that they are human beings. They are to be given ideas; their eyes are to be opened to what is going on in the world around them; and then they will work out their own salvation . . . The great difficulty in the way of educating the poor is this. Supposing even your Highness opens a free school in every village, still it would do no good, for the poverty of India is such that the poor boys would rather go to help their fathers in the fields, or otherwise try to make a living, than come to school. Now if the mountain does not come to Mohammed, Mohammed must go to the mountain. If the poor boy cannot come to education, education must go to him. There are thousands of single-minded, self-sacrificing Sannyāsins in our own country, going from village to village, teaching religion. If some of them can be organised as teachers of secular things also, they will go from place to place, from door to door, not only preaching, but teaching also.[31]

Religion, Politics and Society

In India, religious life forms the centre, the keynote of the whole music of national life; and if any nation attempts to throw off its national vitality — the direction which has become its own through the transmission of centuries — that nation dies if it succeeds in the attempt. And, therefore, if you succeed in the attempt to throw off your religion and take up either politics or society, or any other things as your centre, as the vitality of your national life, the result will be that you will become extinct. To prevent this you must make all and everything work through the vitality of your religion. Let all your nerves vibrate through the backbone of your religion. I have seen that I cannot preach even religion to Americans without showing them its practical effect on social life. I could not preach religion in England without showing the wonderful political changes the Vedanta would bring. So, in India, social reform has to be preached by showing how much more spiritual a life the new system will bring; and politics has to be preached by showing how much it will improve the one thing that the nation wants — its spirituality.[32]

East and West

India and the West

This is the great ideal before us, and every one must be ready for it — the conquest of the whole world by India — nothing less than that, and we must all get ready for it, strain every nerve for it. Let foreigners come and flood the land with their armies, never mind. Up, India, and conquer the world with your spirituality! Ay, as has been declared on this soil first, love must conquer hatred, hatred cannot conquer itself. Materialism and all its miseries can never be conquered by materialism. Armies when they attempt to conquer armies only multiply and make brutes of humanity. Spirituality must conquer the West. Slowly they are finding out that what they want is spirituality to preserve them as nations.

They are waiting for it, they are eager for it. Where is the supply
to come from? Where are the men ready to go out to every country in the world with the messages of the great sages of India?[33]

Oriental and Occidental

To the Oriental, the world of spirit is as real as to the Occidental is
the world of senses. In the spiritual, the Oriental finds everything
he wants or hopes for; in it he finds all that makes life real to him.
To the Occidental he is a dreamer; to the Oriental the Occidental
is a dreamer playing with ephemeral toys, and he laughs to think
that grown-up men and women should make so much of a handful of matter which they will have to leave sooner or later. Each
calls the other a dreamer. But the oriental ideal is as necessary for
the progress of the human race as is the occidental, and I think it
is more necessary . . . When the Occident wants to learn about the
spirit, about God, about the soul, about the meaning and mystery
of this universe, he must sit at the foot of the Orient to learn.[34]

*From Addresses at the World's Parliament of Religions, Chicago,
September 1893.*

Religion not the Crying Need of India

You Christians, who are so fond of sending out missionaries to
save the soul of the heathen — why do you not try to save their
bodies from starvation? In India, during the terrible famines,
thousands died from hunger, yet you Christians did nothing. You
erect churches all through India, but the crying evil in the East is
not religion — they have religion enough — but it is bread that the
suffering millions of burning India cry out for with parched
throats. They ask us for bread, but we give them stones. It is an
insult to a starving people to offer them religion; it is an insult to a
starving man to teach him metaphysics. In India a priest that
preached for money would lose caste and be spat upon by the
people. I came here to seek aid for my impoverished people, and I
fully realised how difficult it was to get help for heathens from
Christians in a Christian land.[35]

Hinduism

At the very outset, I may tell you that there is no *polytheism* in India. In every temple, if one stands by and listens, one will find the worshippers applying all the attributes of God, including omnipresence, to the images. It is not polytheism, nor would the name henotheism explain the situation . . . Names are not explanations . . .

The tree is known by its fruits. When I have seen amongst them that are called idolaters, men, the like of whom in morality and spirituality and love I have never seen anywhere, I stop and ask myself, 'Can sin beget holiness?' . . .

The Hindus have discovered that the absolute can only be realised, or thought of, or stated, through the relative, and the images, crosses, and crescents are simply so many symbols — so many pegs to hang the spiritual ideas on. It is not that this help is necessary for every one, but those that do not need it have no right to say that it is wrong. Nor is it compulsory in Hinduism.[36]

Common Ground

Much has been said of the common ground of religious unity. I am not going just now to venture on my own theory. But if any one here hopes that this unity will come by the triumph of any one of the religions and the destruction of the others, to him I say, 'Brother, yours is an impossible hope.' Do I wish that the Christian would become Hindu? God forbid. Do I wish that the Hindu or Buddhist would become Christian? God forbid . . .

The Christian is not to become a Hindu or a Buddhist, nor a Hindu or a Buddhist to become a Christian. But each must assimilate the spirit of the others and yet preserve his individuality and grow according to his own law of growth.[37]

NOTES

1 *The Complete Works of Swami Vivekananda*, (Calcutta, 1970) Vol. I, 317 – 8.
2 Ibid., 341.
3 Ibid., 375.
4 Ibid., 388.

5   Ibid., Vol. II, 297.
6   Ibid., 365.
7   Ibid., 382 – 3.
8   Ibid., Vol. III, 278 – 80.
9   Ibid., Vol. IV, 358.
10   Ibid., Vol. V, 187 – 8.
11   Ibid., 313.
12   Ibid., Vol. VI, 17.
13   Ibid., 82.
14   Ibid., 82 – 3.
15   Ibid., Vol. II, 252 – 3.
16   Ibid., 333.
17   Ibid., Vol. VIII, 188.
18   Ibid., 101. From a lecture on the 'Buddha's Message to the World' which
     looks at the way the doctrine of anattā can be related to the Ātman/Brahman
     doctrine.
19   Ibid., Vol. VII, 501.
20   Ibid., 78.
21   Ibid., Vol. II, 326.
22   Ibid., Vol. III, 218.
23   Ibid., 460.
24   Ibid., 246 – 7.
25   Ibid., 245 – 6.
26   Ibid., 293 – 5. From a lecture on 'The Future of India' in which the caste
     dimension is regretted, privilege and exclusivism deplored, and Brahmanic
     duty seen as working for the salvation of the people of India.
27   Ibid., Vol. V, 28 – 9.
28   Ibid., Vol. VI, 394.
29   Ibid., Vol. III, 216.
30   Ibid., Vol. IV, 481.
31   Ibid., 362 – 3.
32   Ibid., Vol. III, 220 – 1.
33   Ibid., 276 – 7.
34   Ibid., Vol. IV, 155 – 6.
35   Ibid., Vol. I, 20.
36   Ibid., 15, 17.
37   Ibid., 24.

REFERENCE

The Complete Works of Swami Vivekananda, Vols I – VIII, Calcutta: Advaita
Ashrama, 1970.

7

MAHADEV GOVIND RĀNADE (1842 – 1901)

Mahārāshtra provided modern India with Brahmin leaders of quality and intellectual distinction whose contribution to the renaissance of Hinduism was significant. They advocated social, economic and religious reforms in response to the challenge of Western thought and prominent among them was Mahadev Govind Rānade.

Born in Kolhapur in 1842 into an orthodox Brahmin family, he showed a propensity for learning from an early age and entered the Elphinstone Institution, Bombay, in 1856 and later the University of Bombay where he graduated in law. He was nominated a Fellow of Elphinstone College in recognition of his intellectual distinction and taught history, literature and economics there from 1868. But it was in law that he made his career and in 1871 he was appointed magistrate and later acting judge in the Government courts at Poona. Prior to his death in 1901, he had attained the position of High Court Judge in Bombay.

Throughout his career he worked for the reform of certain Hindu customs such as child marriage, purdah, and the prohibition of widow-remarriage and intermarriage between castes. His second marriage at the age of 32 to a girl of 12 occasioned the criticism that he had betrayed the cause of social reform which he championed by distinguishing between precept and practice in his own life. The explanation that he had submitted unwillingly to the wishes of his father failed to satisfy his fellow reformers who expected him, as founder of the society for the encouragement of widow remarriage, to adhere to his principles by choosing a suitable widow to remarry.

As a member of the Prārthanā Samāj or Prayer Society, a religious organization similar to the Brahmo Samāj and modelled on it, Rānade supported not only the social reforms already referred to and the abolition of caste distinctions and untouchability, but also such religious reforms as the removal of idol worship and the restoration of the worship of God as Supreme Being. That he was a confirmed theist inclined to the Rāmanuja school of Vedantism, is evident from his address on the 'Philosophy of Indian Theism' and similar essays. In his view, however, the theistic movements of the Brahmo Samāj and Prārthanā Samāj were to be regarded as the latest in a series of protests against religious abuses like idolatry and superstition that had occurred from Vedic times. He thus succeeded in locating these movements squarely within traditional Hinduism rather than regarding them as innovative, foreign impositions. His contention that religious reform meant the purification of Hinduism, not its rejection, meant that orthodox Hindus were wooed rather than alienated and he tried to convince them that he was simply continuing the work of the Marāthā saints.

The economic and political status of India also occupied his mind and he examined the need to introduce agrarian reform, encourage swadeshi and seek legitimate political status through parliamentary representation for the Indian people. He was one of the founders of the Indian National Congress and the Industrial Association of Western India in 1887 and 1890 respectively and it is not without justification that he is referred to as the father of Indian economics. He considered industrialization to be necessary for the improvement of the lot of Indians and the removal of poverty and he discussed the possibility of developing staple industries as an integral part of a comprehensive economic policy for India.

Rānade's careful and constructive approach to India's problems earned him the reputation of a moderate reformer and petitions submitted to the Government from the Sarvajanik Sabha which he had built up into one of the foremost politic societies in Western India, were always carefully considered and sometimes accepted. He recognized the benefits British rule had bestowed on India but he was sufficiently patriotic to realize that the transfer of power from the British to Indians was ultimately inevitable since millions of Indians could not be held permanently in a state of subjugation.

After Rānade's death in 1901, Gokhale spoke of the inspiration he was to young men throughout the country and perhaps no one was more inspired to implement his programme of social and economic reform than Gokhale himself.

MAHADEV GOVIND RĀNADE

Theism

Extracts from an essay on the 'Philosophy of Theism' in which Rānade expounds his view that the three postulates of existence, Man, Nature and Infinite Being, are distinct yet interrelated, many yet one and in harmony with one another.

Man finds that his own existence for a moment of time is not intelligible unless there is a background for it to rest upon. He feels that the flux of things is not intelligible unless it also finds its rest in something which knows no flux. Whether the Infinite Being is potential matter, energy, mind or spirit, there are points on which philosophy has proposed various interpretations and solutions. The mystery surrounding this third postulate of existence is not more enigmatical than what is involved in a right understanding of what constitutes the Ego and the Non-Ego. We cannot comprehend the one more clearly than the other. Each of us can realize the fact that he exists, and that something outside him also exists. His own existence and the existence of the Non-Ego become more intelligible to him when he also learns to realize the existence of the Infinite.

All the errors of superstition, scepticism and mysticism spring up from our inability to keep our hold on the three distinct postulates of existence. We should not either explain away or exaggerate any of them. When we localize God in place or time and connect Him with uncommon particular events or places, superstition creeps in and overturns the balance of our mind. When we exaggerate our own powers we end in mysticism, when we unduly allow nature and her forms to dazzle us, and belittle our capacities, we become sceptical.[1]

The threefold postulates of existence are thus seen to be distinct and yet harmonized together. All attempts to assimilate and reduce them into one absolute existence fail, because they are bound to fail. At the same time, they are not distinct in the sense of being disjointed parts of a mechanical whole. They are one and yet they are many. Nature and man each have definite relations of subordination to the great Infinite which rules over them and harmonizes them, and the discovery of these subordinate relations is the special domain of the philosophy of Theism.[2]

The characteristics of Indian Theism, which have enabled it to maintain its identity, will cling to it through all times. They are first its non-historical character. It is associated with no particular saint or prophet though it has room for reverence to all saints and prophets. It is not bound down to any particular revelation but is open to the best influences of all revelations. With it, revelation is a perpetual stream which never ceases to flow. Above all, Indian Theism is built on the rock of the direct communion of the individual soul with the Soul of the Universe to which it is linked by the tie of faith, hope and love.[3]

Social Reform

Marriage

Extracts from 'The Age of Hindu Marriage' in which texts are quoted in support of female liberty and against child marriages.

Two propositions may safely be laid down in this connection:— Firstly, that the Aryan society of the Vedic, or more properly speaking the Grihya Sutra period presents the institution of marriage in a form which recognized female liberty and the dignity of womanhood in full, very slight traces of which are seen in the existing order of things except, fortunately, in the old Sanskrit ritual which is still recited, and the ceremonies which are still blindly performed; and secondly, that owing to causes which it is not possible to trace, there was a revulsion of feeling, and the Vedic institutions were practically abandoned or ignored, and in their place usages grew up which circumscribed female liberty in various directions and seriously lowered the dignity of woman in the social and family arrangements. By clearly separating the texts relating to each period, the confusion of thought and ideas, which marks all orthodox discussion of these subjects, will be avoided, and the whole history presented in a way at once intelligible and suggestive.[4]

(In Aryan society) Marriage took place in all castes at a comparatively mature age, and the remarriage of widows was not looked down upon as disreputable . . .[5]

These texts leave no doubt that the majority of the Smritis favour the age after twenty-five in the case of males. Only one text fixes the age at eighteen and another at sixteen. The maximum limit is also fixed at fifty . . . All these authorities are thus clearly in favour of late, as against child marriages. Nobody now proposes to wait till twenty-five, though that would not be unreasonable, but surely a proposal to raise the minimum age to eighteen or twenty for males is not an unreasonable concession to the weakness of the Kali Yuga.

To proceed next to the consideration of the age for females. It will be noted that the Sutras laid down no minimum or maximum age limit, but left marriages optional. Those who desired to marry might do so at a time of life signified by the use of the words Kanya, Kumari, Yuwati, Kānta, Nagnika, and Brāhmacharini, which in those days were sufficiently indicative of their being grown-up girls. The way in which the Smriti writers proceeded to restrict this freedom was, firstly, by prohibiting the choice of single or unmarried life to females, secondly, by making it compulsory on fathers or guardians to see their daughters married before puberty at the risk of damnation, and thirdly, by inventing new texts limiting the age significance of the words Kanya, Kumari, Nagnika, &c., used by the Sutra writers. It is a very interesting study to mark the successive stages of this gradual process of restriction and degradation. Notwithstanding this manipulation, it will be seen that the majority of the texts favour the age of twelve or the age of puberty as the marriageable age for girls.[6]

Remarriage of Widows

Written in 1870 when the widow remarriage controversy was at its height this paper, which cites Vedic authorities, relates to the deliberation of the council convened to discuss the issue and the defamation case brought by one of the reformers against one of the orthodox party before the magistrate at Poona.

As the learned judge has so forcibly put it, in seeking this reform, the advocates are only endeavouring to restore the purer institutions of old times. People who are, however, not conversant with the merits of the question, may be misled by the special prominence given to one minor argument in the judgment, namely, that the central period of the Kali age, which is the Yuga proper — Kali-yuga not yet come, and to which alone the prohibitions against re-marriage and other institutions can apply, has not yet commenced, and in fact, it will commence only after some thirty-one thousand years from this date. This special mention of it in the judgment may mislead people into thinking that the advocates have after all a very narrow basis to build their great argument upon, and it is deemed necessary that this false impression should be removed. . . .

The advocates of re-marriage are, however, in a position to make out a much stronger case. They are able to show in the first instance, that the re-marriage of widows has the positive authority of the Shāstras, which Shāstra authorities hold good for all the four Yugas, that is for all time. They are also able to establish, that, allowing the prohibitory texts for the Kali-yuga to be in force now, they only restrict, and do not totally abrogate, the privilege enjoyed before, and that the widow's case falls under the class of the permitted circumstances of distress, in which it is lawful for a woman once married in due form, if she is unable to live a life of single devotion to her deceased husband's memory, to marry another man.[7]

The Status of Women and State legislation

This essay seeks to advocate State legislation in social matters to regulate and minimize evil and to promote progress.

It will be clear from this review (of Indian history) that internal dissensions, the upheaval of non-Aryan races, and the predominance acquired by barbarous Scythian and Mohamedan conquerers, degraded the conditions of the female sex, deprived them of their rights of inheritance and freedom, and made woman dependent on man's caprice, instead of being his equal and honoured helpmate. Political and ethnic agencies of great power have wrought the evil, and we cannot afford to lose sight of this fact in our attempts of elevate the status of the female sex. Fortunately, the causes which brought on the degradation have been counteracted by Providential guidance, and we have now, with a living example before us of how pure Aryan customs, unaffected by barbarous laws and patriarchal notions, resemble our own ancient usages, to take up the thread where we dropped it under foreign and barbarous pressure, and restore the old healthy practices, rendered so dear by their association with our best days, and justified by that higher reason which is the sanction of God in man's bosom.

The next question is . . . a more difficult one to deal with. How this gentle revolution is to be effected without breaking with the past, is a problem which admits of differences of views. There are two schools of thinkers among those who have discussed this subject. One set would utilize all the active and passive agencies which tend to encourage and vitalize reform; the other set would leave things to take their own course, firm in the confidence that the passive agencies at work would secure all our ends just as we desire, slowly but surely. Those who feel the full force of the ethnical and political causes mentioned above, and also feel how necessary it is at certain stages of man's progress to secure the assertion of right ideas by the highest sanctions, advocate to some extent the help of State regulation, as representing the highest and most disinterested wisdom of the times, working to give effect to the other tendencies, concentrating and popularizing them. Those who are not sufficiently alive to these considerations would trust to education and the gradual development of better ideas by their own internal force, to achieve all that we desire. It is needless to state that the publication to which these remarks are prefaced is intended to strengthen the hands of the first set of thinkers, and to show, by the examples of what occurred in the past, that timely State regulation is not attended with the mischiefs which people attribute to it, and that it co-ordinates and vivifies the healthy action of other agencies. . .

Whenever there is a large amount of unredressed evil suffered by people who cannot adopt their own remedy, the State has a function to regulate and minimize the evil, if by so regulating it, the evil can be minimized better than by individual effort and without leading to other worse abuses. The State in its collective capacity represents the power, the wisdom, the mercy and charity, of its best citizens. What a single man, or combination of men, can best do on their own account, that the State may not do, but it cannot shirk its duty if it sees its way to remedy evils, which no private combination of men can check adequately or which it can deal with more speedily and effectively than any private combination of men can do. In these latter cases, the State's regulating action has its sphere of duty marked out clearly. On this, and on this principle alone, can State action be justified in many important departments of its activity, such as the enforcement of education, sanitation, factory legislation, of State undertakings like the postal service, or subsidies given to private effort in the way of railway extension and commercial development. The regulation of marriageable age has in all countries, like the regulation of the age of minority, or the fit age for making contracts, been a part of its national jurisprudence, and it cannot be said with justice that this question lies out of its sphere. The same observation holds true of the condition of the widow rendered miserable in early life, and thrown helpless on the world.[8]

Reformation or Revivalism

In an address delivered at the Indian National Social Conference held at Amraoti in 1897 Rānade emphasized the need for reform and indicated the folly of revivalism.

On the other side, some of our orthodox friends find fault with us, not because of the particular reforms we have in view, but on account of the methods we follow. While the new religious sects condemn us for being too orthodox, the extreme orthodox section denounce us for being too revolutionary in our methods. According to these last, our efforts should be directed to revive, and not to reform. I have many friends in this camp of extreme orthodoxy, and their watchword is that Revival, and not Reform, should be our motto. They advocate a return to the old ways, and appeal to the old authorities, and the old sanctions. Here also, as in the instance stated above, people speak without realizing the full significance of their own words. When we are asked to revive our old institutions and customs, people seem to me to be very much at sea as to what it is they seek to revive. What particular period of our history is to be taken as the old — whether the period of the Vedas, of the Smritis, of the Puranas, or of the Mohamedans or the modern Hindu times. Our usages have been changed from time to time by a slow process of growth, and in some cases of decay and corruption, and you cannot stop at any particular period without breaking the continuity of the whole. When my revivalist friend presses his argument upon me he has to seek recourse to some subterfuge which really furnishes no reply to his own question. What shall we revive? Shall we revive the old habits of our people when the most sacred of our castes indulged in all the abominations, as we now understand them, of animal food and intoxicating drink, which exhausted every section of our country's Zoology and Botany . . . Shall we revive the Niyoga system of propagating sons on our brother's wives when widowed? . . . Shall we revive the Shakti worship of the left hand, with its indecencies and practical debaucheries? Shall we revive the *Sati* and infanticide customs, or the flinging of living men into the rivers or over rocks, or hookswinging, or the crushing beneath the Jagannath car? Shall we revive the internecine wars of the Brahmins and Kshatriyas or the cruel persecution and degradation of the Aboriginal population? . . . These instances will suffice to show that the plan of reviving the ancient usages and customs will not work our salvation, and is not practicable. If these usages were good and beneficial, why were they altered by our wise ancestors? If they were bad and injurious, how can any claim be put forward for their restoration after so many ages? Besides, it seems to be forgotten that in a living organism, as society is, no revival is possible.[9]

I think I have said more than enough to suggest to your reflecting minds what it is that we have to reform. All admit that we have been de-formed. We have lost our stature, we are bent in a hundred places, our eyes lust after forbidden things, our ears desire to hear scandals about our neighbours, our tongue wants to taste forbidden fruit, our hands itch for another man's property, our bowels are deranged with indigestible food. We cannot walk on our feet, but require stilts or crutches. This is our present social polity, and now we want this deformity to be removed, and the only way to remove it is to place ourselves under the discipline of better ideas and forms such as those I have briefly touched above. Now this is the work of the reformer. Reforms in the matter of infant marriages and enforced widowhood, in the matter of temperance and purity, intermarriages between castes, the elevation of the low castes, and the readmission of converts, and the regulations of our endowments and charity are reforms, only so far and no further, as they check the influence of the old ideas and promote the growth of the new tendencies. The reformer has to infuse in himself the light and warmth of nature and he can do it by purifying and improving himself and his surroundings.[10]

Common Ground

From an address delivered at the Indian National Social Conference held at Lucknow in 1899 entitled 'I am neither Hindu nor Mahomedan'.

If the lessons of the past have any value, one thing is quite clear, viz., that in this vast country, no progress is possible unless both Hindus and Mahomedans join hands together, and are determined to follow the lead of the men who flourished in Akbar's time, and were his chief advisers and councillors, and sedulously avoid the mistakes which were committed by his great-grandson Aurangzeb. Joint action from a sense of common interest, and a common desire to bring about the fusion of the thoughts and feelings on men, so as to tolerate small differences and bring about concord — these were the chief aims kept in view by Akbar, and formed the principle of the new divine faith formulated in the Din-i-Ilahi. Every effort on the part of either Hindus or Mahomedans to regard their interests as separate and distinct, and every attempt made by the two communities to create separate Schools and interests among themselves, and not to heal up the wounds inflicted by mutual hatred of caste and creed, must be deprecated on all hands. It is to be feared that this lesson has not been sufficiently kept in mind by the leaders of both communities in their struggle for existence, and in the acquisition of power and predominance during recent years. There is at times a great danger of the work of Akbar being undone by losing sight of this great lesson which the history of his reign and that of his two successors is so well calculated to teach. The Conference which brings us together is especially intended for the propagation of this 'Din' or 'Dharma', and it is in connection with that message chiefly that I have ventured to speak to you today on this important subject. The ills that we are suffering are, most of them, self-inflicted evils, the cure of which is to a large extent in our own hands. Looking at the series of measures which Akbar adopted in his time to cure these evils, one feels how correct was his vision when he and his advisers put their hand on those very defects in our natural character, which need to be remedied first before we venture on higher enterprises. Pursuit of high ideals, mutual sympathy and co-operation, perfect tolerance, a correct understanding of the diseases from which the body politic is suffering, and an earnest desire to apply suitable remedies — this is the work cut out for the present generation. The awakening has commenced, as is witnessed by the fact that we are met in this place from such distances for joint consultation and action. All that is needed is that we must put our hands to the plough, and face the strife and the struggle . . .

Both Hindus and Mahomedans have their work cut out in this struggle. In the backwardness of female education, in the disposition to overleap the bounds of their own religion, in matters of temperance, in their internal dissensions between castes and creeds, in the indulgence of impure speech, thought, and action on occasions when they are disposed to enjoy themselves, in the abuses of many customs in regard to unequal and polygamous marriages, in the desire to be extravagant in their expenditure on such occasions, in the neglect of regulated charity, in the decay of public spirit in insisting on the proper management of endowments, — in these and other matters both communities are equal sinners, and there is thus much ground for improvement on common lines.[11]

Hindu Protestantism and Image worship

The Protestant reformers in Europe achieved another change of great importance in the way in which they raised their voice against the excesses to which image-worship and saint-worship were carried in the Roman Catholic Church. On our side, also, this protest was raised, but it did not assume the iconoclastic form which the Protestant reformers, especially the stricter sect among them, adopted. Polytheistic worship was condemned both in theory and in practice by the saints and prophets of Mahārāshtra. Each of them had his own favourite form of the divine incarnation, and this worship of one favourite form left no room for allegiance to other gods . . .

The supremacy of one God, One without a second, was the first article of the creed with every one of these saints, which they would not allow anybody to question or challenge. At the same time, as observed above, the iconoclastic spirit was never characteristic of this country, and all the various forms in which God was worshipped were believed to merge finally into one Supreme Providence or *Brahma*. This tendency of the national mind was a very old tendency. Even in Vedic times, Indra and Varun, Marut and Rudra, while they were separately invoked at the sacrifices offered for their acceptance, were all regarded as interchangeable forms of the One and supreme Lord of creation.

This same tendency explains the comparative indifference with which the saints and prophets treated the question of image-worship. It is a complete misunderstanding if their thoughts and ideas on this subject when it is represented that these gifted people were idolaters in the objectionable sense of the word. They did not worship sticks and stones. In Vedic times there was admittedly no idol or image worship. It came into vogue with the acceptance of the incarnation theory, and was stimulated by the worship of the Jains and Buddhists of their saints. Finally, it got mixed up with the fetish worship of the aboriginal tribes, who were received into the Aryan fold, and their gods were turned into incarnations of the Aryan deities. The saints and prophets, however, rose high above these grovelling conceptions prevalent amongst the people. Idol worship was denounced when the image did not represent the Supreme God.[12]

NOTES

1   M.G. Rānade, *Religious and Social Reform. A Collection of Essays and Speeches by Mahadeva Govind Ranade. Collected and Compiled by M.B. Kolasker.* (Bombay, 1902), 6 – 7.
2   Ibid., 17.
3   Ibid., 24.
4   Ibid., 29.
5   Ibid., 30.
6   Ibid., 40 – 1.
7   Ibid., 54 – 6.
8   Ibid., 100 – 4.
9   Ibid., 169 – 71.
10 Ibid., 176 – 8.
11 Ibid., 246 – 8.
12 Ibid., 220 – 2.

REFERENCE

M.G. Rānade, *Religious and Social Reform. A Collection of Essays and Speeches by Mahadeva Govind Ranade. Collected and Compiled by M.B. Kolasker.* Bombay: Gopal Narayan and Co., G. Claridge and Co., 1902.

8

BĀL GANGĀDHAR TILAK (1856 – 1920)

A son of Mahārāshtra, Tilak was born in the village of Chikalgaon in 1856 and as a Chitpavan Brahman was an officially recognized leader in the community. He inherited all his father's property at the age of sixteen and consequently was relieved of all financial worries. He was educated at Deccan and Elphinstone Colleges concentrating on legal studies. In 1880 he founded a private school in Poona with Vishnu Chiplunkar, Mahadev Ballal Namjoshi and Gopal Ganesh Agarkar. Later with Agarkar he began publishing two weekly newspapers, *Mahratta* in English and *Kesari* in Marāthī, both criticizing the government's system of education and promoting nationalist ideals. A lawsuit filed against them by the diwan of Kolhapur State for defamation resulted in a four months' jail sentence but at the same time won them the sympathy and support of their fellow-countrymen.

The success of the private school led to the establishment of the Deccan Educational Society and in due course to the foundation of Fergusson College as an institution of higher learning in Poona in 1885. Here Tilak and Agarkar were joined by Gokhale who shared in the teaching of mathematics and whose gentle spirit and benign temperament contrasted strongly with the more robust and turbulent temperament of Tilak. Differences of opinion between Tilak and his colleagues Agarkar and Gokhale led ultimately to his resignation from the Deccan Educational Society in 1890.

These differences of opinion are no more clearly seen than in connection with the education of women. Tilak took the orthodox Hindu stance maintaining that the woman's role was to care for the home and that education would only serve to make her discontented with her lot and in some cases disobedient to her husband. When in 1891 the government moved a bill to raise the marriageable age of consent from ten to twelve years Tilak argued that a foreign government should not be allowed to regulate on Hindu social customs and ways of life and that Hindus should be allowed to frame their own rules by voluntary agreement. It was this kind of attitude that led Tilak being called a social reactionary.

From 1891 onwards Tilak devoted his energies to establishing a political movement in Mahārāshtra with a religious base. This was to win him the title of Lokamānya (Revered of the People). His first book *The Orion* sought to prove the antiquity of the Vedas by means of astronomical data in order that the Aryans might be credited with planting the seeds of civilization in the world. His revival and sponsorship of the Ganapti festivals, a ten-day celebration in honour of Ganesh or Ganapti the elephant-headed god, was in direct opposition to the Muslim Mohurram festival held a week earlier and which, until 1893, had been celebrated jointly by Muslims and Hindus. The boycott of the Muslim festival in favour of the resuscitated Hindu festival, while it served to strengthen Hindu consciousness and awaken nationalistic feelings, also sowed the seeds of communal discontent. Tilak's support for the work of the Cow-Preservation Societies, whose activities Muslims considered to be excessively zealous, fanned further the flames of communal unrest. These activities, coupled with his sponsorship of the Shivaji festival and his inflammatory articles in *Kesari*, lend weight to the claim that Tilak made no distinction between religion and politics and was the father of Indian unrest.

Tilak's role in the assassination of two British officers, Walter Charles Rand and Charles Egerton Ayerst, has never been established but his indirect influence through his editorials and speeches is another matter. Official fear and anger led to his arrest in Bombay in 1897 on a charge of exciting feelings of disaffection against the government by his *Kesari* articles. During his trial the competence of his European accusers to understand the nuances of his Marathi articles was questioned — a political as much as a linguistic protest. The six Europeans on the jury returned a verdict of guilty and three Indians a verdict of not guilty. He was sentenced to prison for eighteen months and his appeal against the sentence was rejected.

Tilak saw Hinduism as the unifying factor of Indian society and strove incessantly for the restoration of Hindu orthodoxy. He denounced Western secular education for its indifference to Hindu religion and neglect of morality. His fight for political independence reflects his concern for the protection of the Aryan religion and it is significant that in supporting swadeshi and indigenous industrial development he refers to abstention from the purchase of foreign goods as the 'religion of boycott'. The interrelation of religion and politics in Tilak's militant nationalism meant that his views on education, involving the establishment of an independent Hindu University and a national language, and swadeshi, reflected strong religious convictions. He saw religion as an important element in nationalism and he stirred the hearts of the people with such nationalist slogans as 'swarajya is my birthright and I will have it' and with his exhortations to action on the grounds that the Ganges of independence was the ultimate goal in politics as pilgrimages to Benares were the ultimate goal in religion.

In 1908 Tilak was again arrested in Bombay and accused of expressing seditious ideas in his *Kesari* editorials and condoning political assassination. The European majority on the jury found him guilty and sentenced him to be deported to Mandalay in Burma for six years. Strikes in mills throughout the country ensued, a remarkable testimony to his popular influence. During his period of incarceration his militant philosophy changed and he came to advocate more moderate tactics for the achievement of India's legitimate goals. He spent his time in exile reading books and writing his *Gītā Rahasya* (*The Secret meaning of the Gītā*) in which he stressed disinterested action (karma) rather than devotion (bhakti) or renunciation (saṁyāsa) as the central teaching of the Gita. As a man of action himself it was natural that he should have decried quietism and regarded selfless action as the primary way to moksha. His stress on motive rather than the fruits of action meant also that implicitly if not explicitly he considered violence committed in a just cause to be morally justified.

It was a more moderate Tilak, however, who was released from prison exile in 1914 to the delight of thousands of his followers. He still advocated independence for India but regarded co-operation with the government rather than direct opposition to it to be the more effective means of bringing it about. It was this approach which dominated his statements and actions until his death in 1920.

BĀL GANDĀDHAR TILAK

The Political Situation

From a speech delivered at Calcutta, under the presidency of Bubu Motilal Ghose on 7 June 1906.

Mr. Chairman and Gentlemen, — I am unable to impress you with my feelings and sentiment. I express my gratefulness on my own behalf and that of my friends for the splendid reception accorded to us. This reception is given not to me personally but as a representative of the Marathi nation. This honour is due to the Marathi nation for the services and sympathy towards the Bengali race in their present crisis. The chairman has said that times have altered and I add that the situation is unique. India is under a foreign rule and Indians welcomed the change at one time. Then many races were the masters and they had no sympathy and hence the change was welcomed and that was the cause why the English succeeded in establishing an empire in India. Men then thought that the change was for their good. The confusion which characterised native rule was in striking contrast with the constitutional laws of the British Government. The people had much hope in the British Government, but they were much disappointed in their anticipations. They hoped that their arts and industries would be fostered under British rule and they would gain much from their new rulers. But all those hopes had been falsified. The people were now compelled to adopt a new line, namely, to fight against the bureaucracy.

Hundred years ago it was said, and believed by the people, that they were socially inferior to their rulers and as soon as they were socially improved they would obtain liberties and privileges. But subsequent events have shown that this was not based on sound logic. Fifty years ago Mr. Dadabhai Naoroji, the greatest statesman of India, thought that Government would grant them rights and privileges when they were properly educated, but that hope is gone. Now it might be said that they were not fitted to take part in the administration of the country owing to their defective education. But, I ask, whose fault it is. The Government has been imparting education to the people and hence the fault is not theirs but of the Government. The Government is imparting an education to make the people fit for some subordinate appointments. Professions have been made that one day the people would be given a share in the administration of the country. This is far from the truth. What did Lord Curzon do? He saw that this education was becoming dangerous and he made the Government control more strict. He passed the Universities Act and thus brought all schools under Government control. Education in future would pin the people to service only and they now want to reform it.[1]

Honest Swadeshī

From a speech delivered on Sunday, 23 December 1906 in Beadon Square, Calcutta, under the presidency of Lala Lajpat Rai.

Lord Minto opened the Industrial Exhibition here the other day and, in doing so, said that honest Swadeshism should be dissociated from political aspirations. In other words the Swadeshi agitation had, within the last eighteen months, been carried on by the workers for motives other than those professed and for ends not yet disclosed. This is entirely an unfair representation of the existing state of things and can easily be demonstrated to be so. To begin with, if Lord Minto thinks the Swadeshi workers dishonest, why should he have associated himself with them by consenting to open the Exhibition? Further, if Lord Minto is honest, and our Bengal leaders who have been preaching the Swadeshi cause are dishonest, why should they have invited his Lordship to do the formal and the ceremonious act of declaring the Exhibition open? So taken either way, it will appear that his Lordship and our leaders cannot possibly hit it off together. If he did not want us, we shall certainly be able to do without him. So his consenting to perform the opening ceremony was clearly a great blunder. Then is our movement really dishonest? In Germany, France, America, Governments protect their infant industries by imposing taxes on imports. The Government of India should also have done the same as it professes to rule India in the interests of Indians. It failed in its duty, so the people are trying to do for themselves what the Government ought to have done years and years ago. No, Lord Minto dares not call the Emperor of Germany dishonest nor can he similarly characterise the presidents of the French and American Republics. How then can our leaders be called dishonest? Are they to be abused because they are endeavouring to do what the Government had culpably omitted to do? As head of a despotic Government, his Lordship cannot possibly sympathise with the political aspirations and agitations of the people, and it may be expected that he may maintain an unbroken silence about it. Had I been in his Lordship's position I would have done so, but why should Lord Minto call us dishonest? There is a harder word that is on my lips, but to say the least it is impolitic of Lord Minto to have said so. There it was said that Swadeshi was an industrial movement and has nothing to do with politics. We all know that Government is not engaged in commerce. It might have begun that way but it certainly does not trade now. Did it not protect British trade and adopt measures to promote it? If the Indian Government dissociates itself from the commercial aspirations of the British nation, then it will be time for Swadeshi workers to consider the question of dissociating their movement from politics. But so long as politics and commerce are blended together in this policy of the Government of India, it will be a blunder to dissociate Swadeshi from politics. In fact, Swadeshism is a large term which includes politics and to be a true Swadeshi one must look on all lines — whether political or industrial or economical — which converge our people towards the status of a civilised nation. Gentlemen, I insist on your emphatically repudiating the charge of dishonesty.[2]

Principles of the Nationalist Party

From a speech delivered to a mass meeting of over 3,000 people including the delegates of all provinces at Surat, on the evening of 23 December 1907.

Our aim is self-government. It should be achieved as soon as possible. You should understand this. But the people who brought the Congress to Surat, although Nagpur was willing at any cost, are going to drag the Congress back. We are against autocratic movement. These autocrats want to cripple the Congress and so they are against Boycott and *Swaraj* resolutions. The nation is not for the repressive policy. They don't want to say or rather preach boycott openly. They have no moral courage. They are against the word boycott, they are for Swadeshi. If you are to do it, do not fear. Don't be cowards; when you profess to be Swadeshi you must boycott *videshi* goods; without boycott Swadeshi cannot be practised. If you accept Swadeshi, accept boycott. We want this, 'Don't say what you don't want to do but do what you say.'[3]

Tenets of the New Party

From a speech delivered at Calcutta, 1 January 1907.

Two new words have recently come into existence with regard to our politics, and they are *Moderates* and *Extremists*. These words have a specific relation to time, and they, therefore, will change with time. The Extremists of to-day will be Moderates to-morrow, just as the Moderates of to-day were Extremists yesterday. When the National Congress was first started and Mr. Dadabhai's views, which now go for Moderates, were given to the public, he was styled an Extremist, so that you will see that the term Extremist is an expression of progress. We are Extremists to-day and our sons will call themselves Extremists and us Moderates. Every new party begins as Extremists and ends as Moderates. The sphere of practical politics is not unlimited. We cannot say what will or will not happen 1,000 years hence — perhaps during that long period, the whole of the white race will be swept away in another glacial period. We must, therefore, study the present and work out a programme to meet the present condition.

It is impossible to go into details within the time at my disposal. One thing is granted, viz., that this Government does not suit us. As has been said by an eminent statesman — the government of one country by another can never be a successful, and therefore, a permanent Government. There is no difference of opinion about this fundamental proposition between the Old and New schools. One fact is that this alien Government has ruined the country. In the beginning, all of us were taken by surprise. We were almost dazed. We thought that everything that the rulers did was for our good and that this English Government had descended from the clouds to save us from the invasions of Tamerlane and Chengis Khan, and, as they say, not only from foreign invasions but from internecine warfare, or the internal or external invasions, as they call it. We felt happy for a time, but it soon came to light that the peace which was established in this country did this, as Mr. Dadabhai has said in one place — that we were prevented from going at each other's throats, so that a foreigner might go at the throat of us all. Pax Britannica has been established in this country in order that a foreign Government may exploit the country. That this is the effect of this Pax Britannica is being gradually realised in these days. It was an unhappy circumstance that it was not realized sooner. We believed in the benevolent intentions of the Government, but in politics there is no benevolence.

Benevolence is used to sugar-coat the declarations of self-interest and we were in those days deceived by the apparent benevolent intentions under which rampant self-interest was concealed. That was our state then. But soon a change came over us. English education, growing poverty, and better familiarity with our rulers, opened our eyes and our leaders; especially the venerable leader who presided over the recent Congress was the first to tell us that the drain from the country was ruining it, and if the drain was to continue, there was some great disaster awaiting us. So terribly convinced was he of this that he went over from here to England and spent 25 years of his life in trying to convince the English people of the injustice that is being done to us. He worked very hard. He had conversations and interviews with Secretaries of State, with Members of Parliament — and with what result? He has come here at the age of 82 to tell us that he is bitterly disappointed.

Your industries are ruined utterly, ruined by foreign rule: your wealth is going out of the country and you are reduced to the lowest level which no human being can occupy. In this state of things, is there any remedy by which you can help yourself? The remedy is not petitioning but boycott. We say prepare your forces, organise your power, and then go to work so that they cannot refuse you what you demand. A story in *Mahabharata* tells that Sri Krishna was sent to effect a compromise, but the Pandavas and Kauravas were both organizing their forces to meet the contingency of failure of the compromise. This is politics. Are you prepared in this way to fight if your demand is refused? If you are, be sure you will not be refused; but if you are not, nothing can be more certain than that your demand will be refused, and perhaps, for ever. We are not armed, and there is no necessity for arms either. We have a stronger weapon, a political weapon, in boycott. We have perceived one fact, that the whole of this administration, which is carried on by a handful of Englishmen, is carried on with our assistance. We are all in subordinate service. This whole Government is carried on with our assistance and they try to keep us in ignorance of our power of cooperation between ourselves by which that which is in our own hands at present can be claimed by us and administered by us. The point is to have the entire control in our hands. I want to have the key of my house, and not merely one stranger turned out of it. Self-Government is our goal; we want a control over our administrative machinery. We don't want to become clerks and remain. At present, we are clerks and willing instruments of our own oppression in the hands of an alien Government, and that Government is ruling over us not by its innate strength but by keeping us in ignorance and blindness to the perception of this fact. Professor Seely shares this view. Every Englishman knows that they are a mere handful in this country and it is the business of every one of them to befool you in believing that you are weak and they are strong. This is politics. We have been deceived by such policy so long. What the New Party wants you to do is to realise the fact that your future rests entirely in your own hands. If you mean to be free, you can be free; if you do not mean to be free, you will fall and be for ever fallen. So many of you need not like arms; but if you have not the power of active resistance, have you not the power of self-denial and self-abstinence in such a way as not to assist this foreign Government to rule over you? This is boycott and this is what is meant when we say, boycott is a political weapon. We shall not give them assistance to collect revenue and keep peace. We shall not assist them in fighting beyond the frontiers or outside India with Indian blood and money. We shall not assist them in carrying on the administration of justice. We shall have our own courts, and when time comes we shall not pay taxes. Can you do that by your united efforts? If you can, you are free from to-morrow.[4]

Revolution

From a speech delivered in Marathi at Poona, 25 June 1907, at the Shiva Coronation Festival.

It is true that what we seek may seem like a revolution in the sense that, it means a complete change in the 'theory' of the Government of India as now put forward by the bureaucracy. It is true that this revolution must be a bloodless revolution, but it would be a folly to suppose that if there is to be no shedding of blood there are also to be no sufferings to be undergone by the people. Why, even these sufferings must be great. But you can win nothing unless you are prepared to suffer. The war between selfishness and reason, if it is conducted only with the weapons of syllogism must result in the victory for the former, and an appeal to the good feelings of the rulers is everywhere discovered to have but narrow limits. Your revolution must be bloodless: but that does not mean that you may not have to suffer or to go to jail. Your fight is with bureaucracy who will always try to curb and suppress you. But you must remember that consistently with the spirit of laws and the bloodlessness of the revolution, there are a hundred other means by which you may and ought to achieve your object which is to force the hands of the bureaucracy to concede the reforms and privileges demanded by the people. You must realise that you are a great factor in the power with which the administration in India is conducted. You are yourselves the useful lubricants which enable the gigantic machinery to work so smoothly.

Though down-trodden and neglected, you must be conscious of your power of making the administration impossible if you but choose to make it so. It is you who manage the railroad and the telegraph, it is you who make settlements and collect revenues, it is in fact you who do everything for the administration though in a subordinate capacity. You must consider whether you cannot turn your hand to better use for your nation than drudging on in this fashion. Let your places by filled by Europeans on the splendid salary of eight annas a day if possible. You must seriously consider whether your present conduct is self-respectful to yourselves or useful to the nation.[5]

Self-Government

From a speech on decentralization in which it is advocated that the village be made the unit of self-government.

The village must be made a unit of self-government, and village communities or councils invested with definite powers to deal with all or most of the village questions concerning Education, Justice, Forest, Abkari, Famine Relief, Police, Medical Relief and Sanitation. These units of self-government should be under the supervision and superintendence of Taluka and District Boards which should be made thoroughly representative and independent. This implies a certain amount of definite popular control even over Provincial finance; and the Provincial Contract System will have to be revised not merely to give to the Provincial Government a greater stability and control over its finances, but by further decentralisation to secure for the popular representative bodies adequate assignments of revenue for the aforesaid purposes. This will also necessitate a corresponding devolution of independent legal powers on the popular bodies whether the same be secured by a reform of the Legislative Council or otherwise.

Mere Advisory Councils will not satisfy the aspiration of the people, nor will they remove the real cause of estrangement between the officers and the people. The remedy proposed by me, I know, is open to the objection that it means a surrender of power and authority enjoyed by the bureaucracy at present, and that the efficiency of the administration might suffer thereby. I hold a different view. I think it should be the aim of the British Administration to educate the people in the management of their own affairs, even at the cost of some efficiency and without entertaining any misgiving regarding the ultimate growth and results of such a policy.[6]

Swarāj

From a Home Rule speech at Belgaum, 1 May 1916.

When the people in the nation become educated and begin to know how they should manage their affairs, it is quite natural for them that they themselves should claim to manage the affairs which are managed for them by others . . . And the remedy which is proposed after making inquiries is called Home Rule. Its name is *Swarajya*. To put it briefly, the demand that the management of our affairs should be in our hands is the demand for *Swarajya*.[7]

From a Home Rule speech at Ahmednagar, 31 May 1916.

We have till now made many complaints and Government have heard them; but what is the root of all the complaints? What things come in the way of improving our condition as we desire and what is our difficulty? — this has been considered for about 50 years past, and many wise people have, after due consideration discovered one cause and that is that our people have no authority in their hands. In public matters, different people have different opinions. Some say, 'Do you not possess authority? Do not drink liquor, and all is done.' The advice is sweet indeed, but stopping all the people from drinking liquor cannot be done by mere advice. This requires some authority. He who has not got that authority in his hands cannot do that work. And if it had been possible to do the work by mere advice, then we would not have wanted a king. Government has come into existence for giving effect to the things desired by a large number of people. And as that Government is not in our hands, if anything is desired by thousands of you but not by those who control the administration, that can never be accomplished. I had come here on a former occasion. What about the famine administration of the time? When Government came to know that the weavers sustained great loss during famine no doubt some steps were taken about it. We have lost our trade. We have become mere commission agents. The business of commission agency used to be carried on formerly; it is not that commission agency did not exist before, nor that it does not exist now. The difference is that while at that time you were the commission agents of our trade, you have now become the commission agents of the businessmen of England. You buy cotton here, and send it to England and when the cloth made from it in England arrives, you buy it on commission and sell it to us. The business of commission agency has remained, but what has happened in it is that the profit which this country derived from it, is lost to us and goes to the English. The men and the business are the same. Owing to a change in the ruling power, we cannot do certain things. Such has become the condition that certain things as would be beneficial to the country cannot be carried out. At first we thought that even though the administration was 'alien' it could be prevailed upon to hear. Since the English administration is as a matter of fact 'alien', and there is no sedition in calling it so, there would be no sedition whatever nor any other offence in calling alien those things which are alien. What is the result of the alienness? The difference between aliens and us is that the aliens' point of view is alien, their thoughts are alien, and their general conduct is such that their minds are not inclined to particularly benefit those people to whom they are aliens . . . We want the rule of the English which is over us. But we do not want these intervening middlemen. The grain belongs to the master, the provisions belong to the master. But only remove the intervening middlemen's aching belly, and confer these powers upon the people so that they may duly look to their domestic affairs. We ask for *swarajya* of this kind. This *swarajya* does not mean that the English Government should be removed, the Emperor's rule should be removed and the rule of some one of our Native States should be established in its place. The meaning of *swarajya* is that explained by Mr. Khaparde at Belgaum, viz., we want to remove the priests of the deity. The deities are to be retained. These priests are not wanted. We say, appoint other priests from amongst us. These intervening Collectors, Commissioners and

other people are not wanted, who at present exercise rule over us
. . .

The meaning of the word *swarajya* is Municipal Local Self-
Government. But even that is a farce. It is not sufficient. When an
order comes from the Collector, you have to obey it. He (Collector) has power to call the President and tell him to do such and
such a thing. If the President does not do it, the Collector has
power to remove him. Then where is *swarajya*? (cheers). The
meaning of *swarajya* as stated above is retention of our Emperor
and the rule of the English people, and the full possession by the
people of the authority to manage the remaining affairs. This is
the definition of *swarajya*.[8]

From a Second Home Rule speech at Ahmednagar, 1 June 1916.

If we do not get *swarajya*, there will be no industrial progress. If
we do not get *swarajya* there will be no possibility of having any
kind of education useful to the nation, either primary or higher. If
we do get *swarajya*, it is not merely to advance female education
or secure industrial reform or social reform. All these are parts of
swarajya. Power is wanted first. Where there is power there is
wisdom. Wisdom is not separate from power . . . We are one
nation. We have a duty to perform in this world. We must get the
rights which belong to man by nature. We want freedom. We
must have in our hands the right of carrying on our affairs. If you
do not get these things, no reform would be fruitful to you. That
is the root of all reforms. No power, no wisdom. Mere book
learning is useless. Do you believe that the people who have come
to rule over us are superiors to us in intelligence and learning?
Such is not my own belief. We can show as much learning, as
much courage, as much ability as they. Perhaps they may not be
apparent now, but they are in us.[9]

*From a speech at the Home Rule Conference, Lucknow, 30 December
1916.*

You have to wrest the whole Self-Government from out of the
hands of a powerful bureaucracy. This body has already commenced to work in order to retain power in its own hands. It is but
natural. You would do the same thing yourself if you were in

possession. Possession is nine points of law. Bureaucracy is in possession of power and why should it part with it? Rights cannot be obtained by yearly resolutions. There are difficulties in the way of carrying out these resolutions, but these difficulties must strengthen us in our beliefs and in our actions.

Good done by Bureaucracy

Bureaucracy too have done some good in our country. They have tried to clear India of the jungle that was there. But further on, after clearing the jungle, there is one thing they do. They do not want to sow in the grounds thus cleared. We want to utilise it for agriculture. India has united into one mass under this bureaucracy, now it is expected to rise on the call of duty. The next point naturally arises. We now want liberty. Similarly, we educate our children and expect them to take our position later on in life. So is the case with Englishmen. They have united us, they have educated us and they must expect us to take the position we are fit for. History and reason are against the difficulties created by the bureaucracy and we must triumph in the end. The only thing that comes in our way is that we are not yet prepared. No shillyshallying will do. Be prepared to say that you are a Home Ruler. Say that you must have it and I dare say when you are ready you will get it. There is nothing anarchical in this demand. Are you prepared to work for it?

Home Rule is an extensive subject. A strong resolution has been passed by the Congress and now the education of the masses lies in your hands. Home Rule is the synthesis of all Congress resolutions. Home Rule is the only remedy. Insist on your rights. India is your own house. Is it not? (*Cries of Yes*). Then why not manage it yourself? (*Cheers*). Our domestic affairs must be in our own hands. We do not want separation from England.[10]

From a speech delivered under the presidency of the Honourable Pandit Mada Mohan Malavia, in the compound of the Home Rule League, Allahabad, in October 1917.

One objection raised against Home Rule was that if Home Rule was granted to them they would turn out British people from India. Indians did want English people, English institutions, English liberty and the Empire. But what they said was that the internal administration of India should be under Indian control. English people had it in England, they had it in the colonies and they had it everywhere and would claim it everywhere, and if it was not granted to them they would fight for it, and yet some denied to Indians that right. By whom was this bogey of expelling the English from India raised and for what purpose? That must be clearly understood. It was perhaps understood in this country but it was their business to see that the British people understood it in the right way. Those that held power in their hands at present imagined that Indians were not capable of governing themselves to the limited extent implied by the word Home Rule. They did not tell Indians when they would be able to govern themselves. They did not fix any time limit. Once it used to be said that Asiatic nations were not fit for self-Government. That however was not said now. They now said that India was not now fit for self-Government. If Indians asked them why, they were told that they had not that thing before, they were deficient in education, there were numerous castes quarrelling among themselves, and only British administrators could hold the balance even between rival sections. As regards unfitness he had said something about it the previous day. But it required to be expanded. What was unfitness? Did they mean to say that before the British came here there was no peaceful rule anywhere in India? What was Akbar? Was he a bad ruler? No Englishman could say that. Let them go back to Hindu rule. There were empires of Asoka, Guptas, Rajputs, etc. No history could say that all these empires had managed their states without any system of administration. There were empires in India as big as the German empire and the Italian empire and they were governed peacefully. When peace reigned in the country under the Hindu, Buddhist and Mahomedan rules, what ground was there to say that the descendants of those people who had governed those empires were to-day unfit to exercise that right? There was no disqualification, intellectual or physical which disabled them from taking part in the Government of any empire. They had shown their fitness in the past and were prepared to show it to-day if opportunities were granted to them.[11]

From a Home Rule speech at Akola, January 1917.

Self-Government, as I told you, means Representative Government in which the wishes of the people will be respected and acted upon and not disregarded as now, in the interests of a small

minority of Civil Servants. Let there by a Viceroy and let him be
an Englishman if you like, but let him act according to the advice
of the representatives of the people. Let our money be spent upon
us and with our consent. Let public servants be really servants of
the public and not their masters as they at present are. The question as to how many members will sit in this Council is imma-
terial. The material question is, will the greater majority of them
represent the Indian public or not, and will they be able to dictate
the policy of the Government or not? This then is what Home
Rule really means.[12]

*From a Speech at a Home Rule Conference at Cawnpore, January
1917.*

Now one aspect of Home Rule is to encourage you to acquire the
freedom which you enjoyed in these various departments of life
and to come up to that standard by the co-operation of and under
the sovereignty of the British rule. This result is not to be achieved
by any unlawful and unconstitional means, but I am sure by a
desire and interest to raise your status to achieve this goal by
means of the sympathy of the British people and by remaining a
permanent part of the Empire . . . Home Rule is nothing else, but
to be masters of your houses. Have you ever thought of such a
simple question, 'what am I in my house — am I a dependent or
am I master?' And if India is your house I want to ask you,
gentlemen, whether there can be any ground or reason to tell you
that you ought to be masters so far as your domestic affairs are
concerned. When an Englishman has been deprived of his rights
he will not be content unless he gets back his rights. Why should
you lag behind, why should you not in the name of religion, in the
name of polity, in the name of that polity, which was cultivated in
the past to the largest extent the history of the world has yet produced — in the name of that philosophy that is religious, I appeal
to you to awaken to your position and do your level best for the
attainment of your birth-right — I mean the right of managing
your own affairs in your own home.[13]

Education

A National Education Speech delivered in Marathi at Barsi, 1908.

And in the end we have come to the conclusion that for proper education national schools must be started on all sides. There are some of our private schools but owing to the fear of losing the grant-in-aid, the necessary education cannot be given there. We must start our own schools for this education. We must begin our work selflessly. Such efforts are being made all over the country. The Gurukul of Hardwar stands on this footing. Berar and Madras have also begun to move in this direction. Our *Maharashtra* is a little backward. A few efforts are being made here also; but they need encouragement from you. Money is greatly needed for this work. I am sure, if you realise the necessity and importance of this subject, you would encourage the organisers generously. So far I have told you about the subject, now I turn to tell you what we shall do in these schools of national education.

Of the many things that we will do there *religious education will first and foremost engage our attention.* Secular education only is not enough to build up character. Religious education is necessary because the study of high principles keeps us away from evil pursuits. Religion reveals to us the form of the Almighty. Says our religion that a man by virtue of his action can become even a god. When we can become gods even by virtue of our action, why may we not become wise and active by means of our action like the Europeans? Some say that religion begets quarrel. But I ask, 'Where is it written in religion to pick up quarrels?' If there be any religion in the world which advocates toleration of other religious beliefs and instructs one to stick to one's own religion, it is the religion of the Hindus alone. Hinduism to the Hindus, Islamism to the Musalmans will be taught in these schools. And it will also be taught there to forgive and forget the differences of other religions.

The second thing that we will do, will be to lighten the load of the study of the foreign languages. In spite of a long stay in India no European can speak, for a couple of hours, fluent Marathi, while our graduates are required as a rule to obtain proficiency in the English language. One who speaks and writes good English is said, in these days, to have been educated. But a mere knowledge of the language is no true education. Such a compulsion for the study of foreign languages does not exist anywhere except in India. We spend twenty or twenty-five years for the education which we can easily obtain in seven or eight years if we get it through the medium of our vernaculars. We cannot help learning English; but there is no reason why its study should be made compulsory. Under the Mahomedan rule we were required to learn Persian but we were not compelled to study it. To save unnecessary waste of time we have proposed to give education through our own vernaculars.

We do not get this sort of education for want of self-Government. We should not therefore await the coming of these rights, but we must get up and begin the work.[14]

From a speech given at Benares, at the Nagari Pracharni Sabha Conference, December 1905.

It is part and parcel of a larger movement, I may say a National Movement to have a common language for the whole of India; for a common language is an important element of nationality.[15]

From a speech given at Benares, 3 January 1906.

The idea of a Hindu University where our old religion will be taught along with modern science is a very good one and should have the support of all.[16]

From an article written for New India *expressing views on National Education.*

Where the people and the Government are one, that is, actuated by the same ideals of citizenship, there can arise no conflict or differences of opinion in the matter of National Education. But where the people and the Government have different ideals of citizenship before them, where the governing class wants to keep the people down in spite of their desire to rise to the status of full citizenship in the Empire, there arises the necessity of National Education as distinguished from governmental education. Viewed in this light, National Education is only a branch or a means to the attainment of Self-Government, and those who demand Home Rule for India cannot but zealously support a movement for the establishment of National Education in this country. The conflict which I have mentioned above can only cease when the people and the Government become one on the higher plane of Self-Government. Till then the authorities will, more or less, come in the way of National Education. But these difficulties must be overcome until National Education becomes the ideal of the governing class, which can be the case only when the Government is popularised.[17]

NOTES

1   *Bal Gangadhar Tilak. His Writings and Speeches*, (Madras, 1922) 42 – 3.
2   Ibid., 52 – 4.
3   Ibid., 376 – 7.
4   Ibid., 55 – 7, 63 – 5.
5   Ibid., 76 – 8.
6   Ibid., 94 – 5.
7   Ibid., 117 – 8.
8   Ibid., 140 – 8.
9   Ibid., 164 – 5.
10   Ibid., 208 – 9.
11   Ibid., 254 – 5.
12   Ibid., 213.
13   Ibid., 220 – 2.
14   Ibid., 83 – 6.
15   Ibid., 27.
16   Ibid., 41.
17   Ibid., 368.

REFERENCE

Bal Gangadhar Tilak, His Writings and Speeches. Third Edition. Madras: Ganesh and Co., July 1922 (1st edn. 1918; 2nd enlarged edn. 1919).

9

GOPĀL KRISHNA GOKHALE (1866 – 1915)

Like Rānade and Tilak, Gokhale was a Maharashtrian and shared with them the cultural heritage and traditions of the Marāthī speaking people. A Chitpavan Brahaṁ, he inherited the legacy of leadership within Mahārāshtra that belonged to the Chitpavan community and worked closely with Rānade whom he regarded as his mentor. Born in Kotaluk in 1866 he attended Rajaram College where he was active in raising money for the defence of Agarkar and Tilak in a lawsuit filed against them by the diwan of Kolhapur. Later he transferred to Deccan College where he is reputed to have been a shy but diligent student with a love of poetry and English literature. His final years of study were spent at Elphinstone College in Bombay and on completion of his course he joined Agarkar and Tilak at the new English school in Poona and later shared the teaching of mathematics with Tilak at Fergusson College founded by the Deccan Education Society in 1885. Gentle in spirit, sensitive and soft spoken, Gokhale earned the respect of his students for his warmth and kindness, and his temperament fitted him for his careful, considered and moderate approach to social and political reform.

His difference in temperament from Tilak may have been responsible for their conflicts at Fergusson College and is clearly reflected in their different attitudes to Rānade. Gokhale revered Rānade as his teacher and guru and admired and respected his constructive approach to India's social problems. Tilak's editorial attacks on Rānade for his support of social reforms sponsored by the British government only served to deepen the rift between him and Gokhale. Their differences are also reflected in their attitude to female education which Gokhale saw as the only way to emancipate women from their bondage to degrading ways of life while Tilak believed the woman's place to be in the home.

Gokhale's attitude to education displayed his trust in its liberating power. Given the choice between Western learning and ignorance and superstition for the people of India he chose the former. He moved a resolution against the reduction of government expenditure on education at a meeting of the Bombay Provincial Conference of Congress in 1889. His concern for the well-being of his fellow-countrymen is further reflected in his advocacy of industrialization and his plea to the government to support Indian industries in order that the people of India might prosper. It finds expression also in his resolution concerning Home Military Charges at the Lahore Congress in 1893 where he argued that the charge of £5,000,000 per annum for expenses incurred by the Indian Office and the Indian Army in England was excessive and that the people of India were entitled to ask for redress. In pursuit of this aim he recommended to a royal commission set up to examine the problem that legislation be passed to prevent Indian revenue being used for military purposes outside India.

The financial burden was not the only burden imposed on the people of India. They suffered also the ignominy of being forced to live in an atmosphere of inferiority without the moral uplift of self-respect that is the lot of all self-governing people. Gokhale sought to remedy this through his efforts in the Bombay Legislative Council to which he was elected in 1899, and in the Supreme Legislative Council in Calcutta from 1901. His constructive criticism of the Government's taxation policy which inflicted an intolerable burden on the mass of the people of India was a model of constitutional opposition to foolish legislation through reasoned arguments, and his appeal for a comprehensive programme to promote the moral and material well-being of the Indian people through industrial and educational advancement produced concessions for his fellow-countrymen. In pursuit of his remedial aims he founded also the Servants of India Society to prepare Indians for leadership in a self-governing nation. Modelled on the Roman Catholic Society of Jesus and the order of Hindu ascetics founded by Ramdas, the aim of the Society was to promote the national interests of the Indian people by constitutional means. It sought the educational advancement of all classes, the cultivation of political awareness, industrial development, the elevation of the depressed classes and the promotion of goodwill and love of India. The fact that in Gokhale's view a self-governing India could remain within the British Empire illustrates his belief in the providential nature of British rule in India. It may account also for his approval of swadeshi but not of the boycott of British goods since the former enshrined the spirit of patriotism while the latter simply provoked angry passions. His differences with Tilak on this subject reflect the essential difference between the moderate and extremist approaches to social and political reforms. Gokhale's goal was self-government for India through constitutional methods which would retain the good-will and co-operation of the British people.

GOPĀL KRISHNA GOKHALE

Social Reforms

Depressed Classes

At the Dharwar Social Conference held on 27 April 1903, Gokhale moved the following resolution on the elevation of the depressed classes:

That this Conference holds that the present degraded condition of the low castes is in itself and from the national point of view unsatisfactory, and is of the opinion that every well-wisher of the country should consider it his duty to do all he can to raise the moral and social condition by trying to rouse self-respect in these classes and placing facilities for education and employment within their reach.

Gentlemen, I hope I am not given to the use of unnecessarily strong language and yet I must say that this resolution is not as strongly worded as it should have been. The condition of the low castes — it is painful to call them low castes — is not only unsatisfactory as this resolution says — it is so deeply deplorable that it constitutes a grave blot on our social arrangements; and, further, the attitude of our educated men towards this class is profoundly painful and humiliating. I do not propose to deal with this subject as an antiquarian; I only want to make a few general observations from the standpoint of justice, humanity, and national self-interest. I think all fair-minded persons will have to admit that it is absolutely monstrous that a class of human beings, with bodies similar to our own, with brains that can think and with hearts that can feel, should be perpetually condemned to a low life of utter wretchedness, servitude and mental and moral degradation, and that permanent barriers should be placed in their way so that it should be impossible for them ever to overcome them and improve their lot. This is deeply revolting to our sense of justice. I believe that one has only to put oneself mentally into their place to realise how grievous this injustice is. We may touch a cat, we may touch a dog, we may touch any other animal, but the touch of these human beings is pollution! And so complete is now the mental degradation of these people that they see nothing in such

treatment to resent, that they acquiesce in it as though nothing
better than that was their due . . .

How can we possibly realise our national aspirations, how can
our country ever hope to take her place among the nations of the
world, if we allow large numbers of our countrymen to remain
sunk in ignorance, barbarism, and degradation?[1]

Indentured Labour

*From a speech in the Imperial Legislative Council, 25 February 1910,
moving a resolution to prohibit the recruitment of indentured labour
in India for the Colony of Natal.*

Now, my Lord, my own view of this system of indentured labour
is that it should be abolished altogether. It is true that it is not
actual slavery ·but I fear in practice in a large number of cases it
cannot be far removed from it. To take from this country helpless
men and women to a distant land, to assign them there to employ-
ers in whose choice they have no voice and of whose language,
customs, social usages and special civilisation they are entirely
ignorant, and to make them work there under a law which they do
not understand and which treats their simplest and most natural
attempts to escape ill-treatments as criminal offences — such a
system by whatever name it may be called, must really border on
the servile. This is also the view which the entire Indian community throughout South Africa takes of the matter . . .

Let us now glance briefly at the state of things in the Transvaal
. . . Alone among British colonies the Transvaal has sought to
inflict galling and degrading indignities and humiliations on his
Majesty's Indian subjects. The protest which the Indian community of the Transvaal has made against these disabilities and
indignities during the last three years has now attained historic
importance . . . The struggle has not yet ended — the end is not
even in sight.[2]

*From a speech in the Imperial Legislative Council, 4 March 1912, moving
a resolution to prohibit the recruitment of Indian indentured labour for
employment at home or in any British Colony.*

. . . when it is remembered that the victims of the system — I can
call them by no other name — are generally simple, ignorant,

illiterate, resourceless people belonging to the poorest classes of
this country and that they are induced to enter — or it would be
more correct to say are entrapped into entering — into these
agreements by the unscrupulous representations of wily profes-
sional recruiters, who are paid so much per head for the labour
they supply and whose interest in them ceases the moment they
are handed to the emigration agents, no fair-minded man will, I
think, hesitate to say that the system is a monstrous system,
iniquitious in itself, based on a fraud and maintained by force,
nor will he, I think demur to the statement that a system so wholly
opposed to modern sentiments of justice and humanity is a grave
blot on the civilization of any country that tolerates it.[3]

Servants of India

The Servants of India Society will train men prepared to devote
their lives to the cause of the country in a religious spirit, and will
seek to promote, by all constitutional means, the national interests of the Indian people. Its members will direct their efforts
principally towards (1) creating among the people, by example
and by precept, a deep and passionate love of the motherland,
seeking its highest fulfilment in service and sacrifice; (2) organis-
ing the work of political education and agitation, basing it on a
careful study of the country; (3) promoting relations of cordial
goodwill and co-operation among the different communities; (4)
assisting educational movements, especially those for the education of women, the education of backward classes and industrial
and scientific education; (5) helping forward the industrial
development of the country; and (6) the elevation of the depressed
classes.[4]

Nationalism

Swadeshī

*From the presidential address delivered at the Indian National
Congress at Banares in 1905.*

Gentlemen, the true *Swadeshi* movement is both a patriotic and
an economic movement. The idea of *Swadeshi* or 'one's own
country' is one of the noblest conceptions that have ever stirred

the heart of humanity . . . The devotion to motherland, which is enshrined in the highest *Swadeshi*, is an influence so profound and so passionate that its very thought thrills and its actual touch lifts one out of oneself. India needs today above everything else that the gospel of this devotion should be preached to high and low, to prince and peasant, in town and in hamlet, till the service of motherland becomes with us as overmastering a passion as it is in Japan.[5]

From an address delivered at Lucknow, 9 February 1907.

One of the most gratifying signs of the present times is the rapid growth of the Swadeshi sentiment all over the country during the last two years. I have said more than once here, but I think the idea bears repetition, that Swadeshism at its highest is not merely an industrial movement, but that it affects the whole life of the nation — that Swadeshism at its highest is a deep, passionate, fervent, all-embracing love of the mother land, and that this love seeks to show itself, not in one sphere of activity only, but in all; it invades the whole man, and will not rest until it has raised the whole man . . .

Now as our needs are various, so the *Swadeshi* cause requires to be served in a variety of ways, and we should be careful not to quarrel with others simply because they serve the cause in a different way from our own. Thus, whoever tries to spread in the country a correct knowledge of the industrial conditions of the world and points out how we may ourselves advance, is a promoter of the *Swadeshi* cause. Whoever again contributes capital to be applied to the industrial development of the country must be regarded as a benefactor of the country and a valued supporter of the *Swadeshi* movement. Then those who organise funds for sending Indian students to foreign countries for acquiring industrial or scientific education . . . are noble workers in the *Swadeshi* field. These three ways of serving the *Swadeshi* cause are, however, open to a limited number of persons only. But there is a fourth way, which is open to all of us, and in the case of most, it is, perhaps, the only way in which they can help forward the *Swadeshi* movement. It is to use ourselves, as far as possible, *Swadeshi* articles only and to preach to others that they should do the same. By this we shall ensure the consumption of whatever articles are produced in the country, and we shall stimulate the production of new articles by creating a demand for them . . .

In this connection I think I ought to say a word about an expression which has, of late, found considerable favour with a section of my countrymen — 'the boycott of foreign goods'. I am sure that most of those that speak of this 'boycott' mean by it only the use, as far as possible, of *Swadeshi* articles in preference to foreign articles. Now such use is really included in true *Swadeshi*; but unfortunately the word 'boycott' has a sinister meaning — it implies a vindictive desire to injure another, no matter what harm you may thereby cause to yourself. And I think we would do well to use only the word *Swadeshi* to describe our present movement, leaving alone the word 'boycott' which creates unnecessary ill-will against ourselves.[6]

Self-Government

The fact that a small island at one end of the world had by an astonishing succession of events been set to rule over a vast country, inhabited by an ancient and civilised race, at the other end; the character of the new rulers as men who had achieved constitutional liberty for themselves, and who were regarded as friends of freedom all over the world; their noble declarations of policy in regard to India — these were well calculated to cast a spell on the Indian mind . . . The spell, however, is already broken, and even the hold on the reason is steadily slackening. A tendency has set in to depreciate even those advantages which at one time were most cordially acknowledged. And the disadvantages of the situation — wounded self, inability to grow to the full height of one's stature, a steady deterioration in the manhood of the nation, and the economic evils of vast magnitude inseparable from such foreign domination — these evils which, while the spell lasted, had not been realised with sufficient clearness, have now already begun to appear as intolerable . . .

The system under which India is governed at present is an unnatural system, and however one may put up with it as a temporary evil, as a permanent arrangement it is impossible, for under such a system 'the noble, free, virile, fearlesslike', to use the words of a well-known American preacher, 'which is the red blood of any nation gradually becomes torpid', and nothing can compensate a people for so terrible a wrong.[7]

But two things I wish to say for my countrymen. First, that because we came under the rule of foreigners, it does not mean that we are like some savage or semi-civilized people whom you have subjugated. The people of India are an ancient race who had attained a high degree of civilization long before the ancestors of European nations understood what civilization was. India has been the birth place of great religions. She was also the cradle and long the home of literature and philosophy, of science and arts. But God does not give everything to every people, and India in the past was not known for that love of liberty and that appreciation of free institutions which one finds to be so striking a characteristic of the West. Secondly, because the Indians are under the rule of foreigners, it does not follow that they are lacking in what is called the martial spirit; for some of the best troops that fight the battles of the Empire today are drawn from the Indians themselves. I mention these two things because I want you to recognize that though we have lost our independence, we have not, on that account, quite forfeited our title to the respect and consideration of civilized people . . .

According to the last census, there are a million men in India today who have come under the influence of some sort of English education. You cannot hope to keep this large and growing class shut out completely from power, as at present. Even if it were possible to perpetuate the present monopoly of power by the bureaucracy, your national honour demands that such an attempt should not be made.[8]

For the last twenty years the Indian people have been agitating for a greater voice in the affairs of their country, through the Indian National Congress. The bureaucracy, however, pays little attention to what we say in India, and so my countrymen thought it desirable that an appeal should now be addressed direct to the electors of this country. The natural evils inseparable from a foreign bureaucracy monopolising all power have, during the last ten years, been intensified by the reactionary policy of the Indian Government, and this reaction and repression has been darkest during the last three years. You, Sir, have said, and I am glad you have said it, that my personal feeling towards Lord Curzon, on whom the chief responsibility for the repression of the last three years mainly rests, is one of respect. That is so . . . You will find — and I am anxious to be fair to Lord Curzon — that while he has done a great deal of good work in certain directions — giving larger grants to irrigation, to agricultural education, and to primary education, putting down assaults by Europeans on Indians, rousing local governments to greater energy, and so on

— where he had to deal with the educated classes of the country and their legitimate position and aspirations, he has been reactionary, and even repressive. And it is this reaction and this repression that has driven my countrymen to a position bordering on despair . . .

The only solution that is possible — a solution demanded alike by our interests and by your interests, as also by your national honour — is the steady introduction of self-government in India. Substituting the Indian for the English agency, expanding and reforming the Legislative Councils till they become in reality true controlling bodies, and letting the people generally manage their own affairs themselves.[9]

And here at the outset . . . let me say that I recognize no limits to my aspiration for our motherland, I want our people to be in their own country what other people are in theirs. I want our men and women, without distinction of caste or creed, to have opportunities to grow to the full height of their stature, unhampered by cramping and unnatural restrictions. I want India to take her proper place among the great nations of the world, politically, industrially, in religion, in literature, in science and in the arts. I want all this and feel at the same time that the whole of this aspiration can, in its essence and its reality, be realized within this Empire.[10]

The first effect of Western teaching on those who received it was to incline them strongly in favour of the Western way of looking at things, and under this influence they bent their energies, in the first instance, to a re-examination of the whole of their ancient civilisation — their social usages and institutions, their religious beliefs, their literature, their science, their art, in fact, their entire conception and realisation of life. This brought them into violent collision with their own society, but that very collision drove them closer to the Englishmen in the country, to whom they felt deeply grateful for introducing into India the liberal thought of the West, with its protest against caste or sex disabilities and its recognition of man's dignity as man — a teaching which they regarded as of highest value in serving both as a corrective and a stimulant to their old civilisation. On one point they entertained no doubt whatever in their minds. They firmly believed that it was England's settled policy to raise steadily their political status till at last they fully participated in the possession of those free institutions which it is the glory of the English race to have evolved. This belief, so strong at one time, began, however, gradually to weaken, when it was seen that English administrators were not in practice as ready to advance along lines of constitutional development as had been hoped and that the bulk of Englishmen in the country were far from friendly even to the most reasonable aspirations of Indians in political matters . . .

The political evolution to which Indian reformers look forward is representative Government on a democratic basis . . . It is unnecessary to say that it is largely in England's power to hasten or delay this evolution.[11]

Education

From a speech in the Imperial Legislative Council asking permission to introduce a Bill to make better provision for the extension of elementary education in India, 16 March 1911.

Even if the advantages of an elementary education be put no higher than a capacity to read and write, its universal diffusion is a matter of prime importance, for literacy is better than illiteracy any day, and the banishment of a whole people's illiteracy is no mean achievement. But elementary education for the mass of the people means something more than a mere capacity to read and write. It means for them a keener enjoyment of life and a more refined standard of living. It means the greater moral and economic efficiency of the individual. It means a higher level of intelligence for the whole community generally. He who reckons these advantages lightly may as well doubt the value of light or fresh air in the economy of human health. I think it is not unfair to say that one important test of the solicitude of a Government for the true well-being of its people is the extent to which, and the manner in which, it seeks to discharge its duty in the matter of mass education. And judged by this test, the Government of this country must wake up to its responsibilities much more than it has hitherto done, before it can take its proper place among the civilised Governments of the world.[12]

Women and Education

From a paper read at the Educational Congress held in connection with the Women's Education Section of the Victoria Era Exhibition, London, 1897.

A wide diffusion of female education in all its branches is a factor of the highest value to the true well-being of every nation. In India it assumes additional importance by reason of the bondage of caste and custom which tries to keep us tied down to certain fixed ways of life and fixed modes of thought, and which so often cripples all efforts at the most elementary reforms. One peculiarity of the Indian life of the present day is the manner in which almost every single act of our daily life is regarded as regulated by some religious notion or another . . . All who know anything of Indian women know that the turn of their mind is intensely religious — a result due in no small measure to their being shut out from all other intellectual pursuits. And this combination of enforced ignorance and overdone religion not only makes them willing victims of customs unjust and hurtful in the highest degree, but it also makes them the most formidable, because the most effective, opponents of all attempts at change or innovation. It is obvious that, under the circumstances, a wide diffusion of education, with all its solvent influences, among the women of India, is the only means of emancipating their minds from this degrading thraldom to ideas inherited through a long past and that such emancipation will not only restore women to the honoured position which they at one time occupied in India, but will also facilitate, more than anything else, our assimilation of those elements of Western civilisation without which all thoughts of India's regeneration are mere idle dreams, and all attempts at it foredoomed to failure.[13]

Economics

From the Budget Speech delivered at the Imperial Legislative Council, 26 March 1902.

Your Excellency, I fear I cannot conscientiously join in the congratulations which have been offered to the Hon'ble Finance

Member on the huge surplus which the revised estimates show for last year. A surplus of seven crores of rupees is perfectly unprecedented in the history of Indian finance, and coming as it does on top of a series of similar surpluses realised when the country has been admittedly passing through very trying times, it illustrates to my mind in a painfully clear manner the utter absence of a due correspondence beween the condition of the people and the condition of the finances of the country. Indeed, my Lord, the more I think about this matter the more I feel — and I trust your Lordship will pardon me from speaking somewhat bluntly — that these surpluses constitute a double wrong to the community. They are a wrong in the first instance in that they exist at all — that Government should take so much more from the people than is needed in times of serious depression and suffering; and they are also a wrong, because they lend themselves to easy misinterpretation and, among other things, render possible the phenomenal optimism of the Secretary of State for India, who seems to imagine that all is for the best in this best of all lands. A slight examination of these surpluses suffices to show that they are mainly, almost entirely currency surpluses, resulting from the fact that Government still maintain the same high level of taxation which they considered to be necessary to secure financial equilibrium when the rupee stood at its lowest . . .

A taxation so forces as not only to maintain a *budgetary equilibrium* but to yield as well 'large, continuous, progressive surpluses' — even in years of trial and suffering — is, I submit, against all accepted canons of finance . . .

My Lord, the obligation to remit taxation in years of assured surpluses goes, I believe, with the right to demand additional revenues from the people in times of financial embarrassment.[14]

NOTES

1   *Speeches of Gopal Krishna Gokhale*, (Madras, 1920), 898 – 901.
2   Ibid., 510, 514 – 5.
3   Ibid., 520 – 1.
4   Ibid., 915 – 6. From the Constitution of the Servants of India, Poona, 12 June 1905.
5   Ibid., 691.
6   Ibid., 958, 972 – 3.
7   Ibid., 987, 990. From a paper read before the East India Association, London.

8 Ibid., 925, 928. From a speech delivered at the National Liberal Club, London.
9 Ibid., 938 – 9, 945. From a speech delivered to the New Reform Club, London.
10 Ibid., 949. From a speech delivered at a public meeting in Allahabad.
11 Ibid., 1015 – 16, 1021. From a paper read at the Universal Races Congress, London.
12 Ibid., 608.
13 Ibid., 882 – 3.
14 Ibid., 1 – 2, 6, 11.

REFERENCE

Speeches of Gopal Krishna Gokhale. Third Edition. Madras: G.A. Natesan and Co., 1920.

10

RABINDRANĀTH TAGORE (1861 – 1941)

One of fifteen children, Rabindranāth Tagore was the son of Debendranāth Tagore and benefited from being nurtured in a highly religious and cultured environment. His father, a wealthy landowner, was one of the leaders of the Brahmo Samāj and his brothers and sisters showed artistic and literary leanings. Rabindranāth himself displayed poetic tendencies early and by the age of 20 had produced a volume of poems in Bengali. He is reputed to have been influenced by the Bauls, a Bengali religious sect from the lower strata of society which eschewed traditional religious rites and customs and, while stressing naturalness and simplicity, sought to express themselves in devotional songs and cultivate an immediate relationship with God. Their stress on bhakti like that of the Vaiṣṇava poets is reflected in the literary work of Tagore whose contribution to the cultural heritage of India matured with the years, culminating in 1913, a year after the publication of *Gitanjali* (*Song Offering*), in the award of the Nobel prize for literature and a year before his death in the granting of the degree of Doctor of Letters *honoris causa* by Oxford University, a degree conferred on him by Sir Maurice Gwyer and S. Radhakishnan at Shantiniketan.

In pursuit of his religious, cultural and educational ideals, he developed a centre of learning at Shantiniketan which resulted in the establishment of Visva Bharati University in 1921 dedicated to the ideals of universal brotherhood and cultural exchange. The rural nature of the location reflects his views concerning the interrelation of God, man and nature. The Absolute is manifested in creation, hence both man and nature are revelations of God. The same power that creates the universe enlightens man's consciousness and the goal is to realize the Absolute, to attain to the perfection of the infinite, through the immediate apprehension of the divine in one's own soul. Man is aided in this when he recognizes the real significance of nature as permeated and vitalized by the Spirit of God and his own kinship with it. His best means of spiritual progress is through a life lived close to nature, for the most effective means for the cultivation of religious piety is not through the rites and ceremonies of temples of worship but in places of natural beauty where nature and soul are united.

Education, therefore, should not be concerned simply with imparting information or the cultivation of the intellect; it should aim to emancipate the soul and liberate the human spirit and to achieve this end due attention should be paid to both atmosphere and environment and the use of indigenous languages in the development of the whole man.

Man's kinship with nature is coupled with his identity with his fellow man. The immanence of God in creation means that there can be no withdrawal from the world or from the needs of our fellow men. Social justice is the inevitable consequence of divine immanence and nothing can be deemed untouchable in a world suffused by the spirit of God. This means that the rigidity and exclusivism of the caste system must go since it militates against both individual freedom and social justice and is contrary to cultivation of spirituality.

Concern for the nurture of the soul determines Tagore's attitude to industrialization and wealth. Acceptance of the necessity for some form of industrialization for the development of India does not mean abrogating responsibility for the preservation of man's creative spirit. The whole of life must reflect the spirit of religion if man's faculties are not to be stunted and his creativity undermined. The same applies to the selfish pursuit of materialistic goals; when wealth becomes an end in itself man is degraded. What is needed is a healthy concern for the basic requirements of material existence together with a profound respect for spiritual values, that is, a harmonization of the approaches of East and West.

Selfishness on a national level in Tagore's view takes the form of patriotism devoid of concern for humanity as a whole. Imperialism is simply the natural result of selfish nationalism which is not averse to the use of force and aggression to achieve its ends. Religion, with its stress on the importance of spiritual values and human personality, is opposed to such narrow, selfish nationalism and Tagore advocates the type of nationalism that is compatible with religious ideals and promotes the love and unity of mankind. India, he claims, should seek her freedom and independence in order to make her own contribution to the spiritual welfare of all peoples and thereby fulfil her destiny among the nations of the world.

RABINDRANĀTH TAGORE

Religion

The following extracts from Tagore's writings illustrate his view of religion as that which is intimately related to man and nature.

I was born in a family which, at that time, was earnestly developing a monotheistic religion based upon the philosophy of the Upanishad. Somehow my mind at first remained coldly aloof, absolutely uninfluenced by any religion whatever. It was through an idiosyncrasy of my temperament that I refused to accept any religious teaching merely because people in my surroundings believed it to be true. I could not persuade myself to imagine that I had a religion because everybody whom I might trust believed its value . . .

When I was eighteen, a sudden spring breeze of religious experience for the first time came to my life and passed away leaving in my memory a direct message of spiritual reality. One day while I stood watching at early dawn the sun sending out its rays from behind the trees, I suddenly felt as if some ancient mist had in a moment lifted from my sight, and the morning light on the face of the world revealed an inner radiance of joy. The invisible screen of the commonplace was removed from all things and all men, and their ultimate significance was intensified in my mind; and this is the definition of beauty. That which was memorable in this experience was its human message, the sudden expansion of my consciousness in the super-personal world of man.[1]

It is for dignity of being that we aspire through the expansion of our consciousness in a greater reality of Man to which we belong. We realise it through admiration and love, through hope that soars beyond the actual, beyond our own span of life into an endless time wherein we live the life of all men.

This is the infinite perspective of human personality where man finds his religion.[2]

In India, there are those whose endeavour is to merge completely their personal self in an impersonal entity which is without any quality or definition; to reach a condition wherein mind becomes perfectly blank, losing all its activities . . . Without disputing its truth I maintain that it may be valuable as a psychological experience but all the same it is not religion, even as the knowledge of the ultimate state of the atom is of no use to an artist who deals in images in which atoms have taken forms.[3]

Religion consists in the endeavour of men to cultivate and express those qualities which are inherent in the nature of Man the Eternal, and to have faith in him.[4]

All things that had seemed like vagrant waves were revealed to my mind in relation to a boundless sea. I felt sure that some Being who comprehended me and my world was seeking his best expression in all my experiences, uniting them into an ever-widening individuality which is a spiritual work of art.

To this Being I was responsible; for the creation in me is his as well as mine. It may be that it was the same creative Mind that is shaping the universe to its eternal idea; but in me as a person it had one of its special centres of a personal relationship growing into a deepening consciousness . . . I felt that I had found my religion at last, the religion of Man, in which the infinite became defined in humanity and came close to me so as to need my love and co-operation.[5]

Religion is not a fractional thing that can be doled out in fixed weekly or daily measures as one among various subjects in the school syllabus. It is the truth of our complete being, the consciousness of our personal relationship with the infinite; it is the true centre of gravity of our life.[6]

The difference between the spirit and the form of religion, like that between fire and ash, should be borne in mind. When the form becomes more important than the spirit, the sand in the river-bed becomes more pronounced that the water, the current ceases to flow, and a desert is the ultimate result.[7]

It is significant that all great religions have their historic origin in persons who represented in their life a truth which was not cosmic and immoral, but human and good. They rescued religion from the magic stronghold of demon force and brought it into the inner heart of humanity, into a fulfilment not confined to some exclusive good fortune of the individual but to the welfare of all men. This was not for the spiritual ecstasy of lonely souls, but for the spiritual emancipation of all races. They came as the messengers of Man to men of all countries and spoke of the salvation that could only be reached by the perfecting of our relationship with Man the Eternal, Man the Divine.[8]

God and Man

*The divinity of man and the humanity of God is the subject of the
following extracts. The notion of a remote, distant God is rejected.*

The idea of the humanity of our God, or the divinity of Man the
Eternal, is the main subject of this book. This thought of God has
not grown in my mind through any process of philosophical
reasoning. On the contrary, it has followed the current of my
temperament from early days until it suddenly flashed into my
consciousness with a direct vision.[9]

As long as man deals with his God as the dispenser of benefits
only to those of His worshippers who know the secret of pro-
pitiating Him, he tries to keep Him for his own self or for the tribe
to which he belongs. But directly the moral nature, that is to say,
the humanity of God is apprehended, man realizes his divine self
in his religion, his God is no longer an outsider to be propitiated
for a special concession. The consciousness of God transcends the
limitations of race and gathers together all human beings within
one spiritual circle of union.[10]

It may be one of the numerous manifestations of God, the one
in which is comprehended Man and his Universe. But we can
never know or imagine him as revealed in any other conceivable
universe so long as we remain human beings. And, therefore,
whatever character our theology may ascribe to him, in reality he
is the infinite ideal of Man towards whom men move in their
collective growth, with whom they seek their union of love as individuals, in whom they find their ideal of father, friend and
beloved.[11]

In India, the greater part of our literature is religious, because
God with us is not a distant God; He belongs to our homes, as
well as to our temples. We feel this nearness to us in all the human
relationship of love and affection, and in our festivities. He is the
chief guest whom we honour. In seasons of flowers and fruits, in
the coming of the rain, in the fulness of the autumn, we see the
hem of His mantle and hear His footsteps. We worship Him in all
the true objects of our worship and love Him whenever our love is
true. In the woman who is good we feel Him, in the man who is
true we know Him, in our children He is born again and again,
the Eternal Child.[12]

> Leave this chanting and singing and
> telling of beads! Whom dost thou
> worship in this lonely dark corner of a
> temple with doors all shut? Open
> thine eyes and see thy God is not before
> thee!
> He is there where the tiller is tilling
> the hard ground and where the path-
> maker is breaking stones. He is with
> them in sun and in shower, and his
> garment is covered with dust. Put off
> thy holy mantle and even like him come
> down on the dusty soil! [13]

Our union with a Being whose activity is world-wide and who dwells in the heart of humanity cannot be a passive one. In order to be united with Him we have to divest our work of selfishness and become *visvakarma*, 'the world-worker', we must work for all. When I use the words 'for all', I do not mean for a countless number of individuals. All work that is good, however small in extent, is universal in character. Such work makes for a realization of *Visvakarma*, 'the World-Worker', who works for all. In order to be one with this Mahatma, 'the Great Soul', one must cultivate the greatness of soul which identifies itself with the soul of all peoples and not merely with that of one's own. [14]

In the history of man moments have come when we have heard the music of God's life touching man's life in perfect harmony. We have known the fulfilment of man's personality in gaining God's nature for itself, in utter self-giving out of abundance of love. [15]

We are hidden in ourselves, like a truth hidden in isolated facts. When we know that this One in us is One in all, then our truth is revealed.

But this knowledge of the unity of soul must not be an abstraction. It is not that negative kind of universalism which belongs neither to one nor to another. It is not an abstract soul, but it is my own soul which I must realize in others. I must know that if my soul were singularly mine, then it could not be true; at the same time if it were not intimately mine, it would not be real. [16]

What is it in man that asserts its immortality in spite of the obvious fact of death? It is not his physical body or his mental organization. It is that deeper unity, that ultimate mystery in him, which, from the centre of his world, radiates towards its circumference; which is in his body, yet transcends his body; which is in his mind, yet grows beyond his mind; which, through the things belonging to him, expresses something that is not in them; which while occupying his present, overflows its banks of the past and future. It is the personality of man, conscious of its inexhaustible abundance . . .[17]

> He whom I enclose with my name is
> weeping in this dungeon. I am ever
> busy building this wall all around; and
> as this wall goes up into the sky day
> by day I lose sight of my true being in
> its dark shadow.
>
> I take pride in this great wall, and I
> plaster it with dust and sand lest a least
> hole should be left in this name; and
> for all the care I take I lose sight of
> my true being.[18]

Education

Tagore emphasizes the study of the mother tongue as a condition for the development of personality; the importance of integrated study in the context of nature; the harmonious development of all the faculties in a residential setting; and the combination of nationalism and internationalism.

The power of thought and the power of imagination are indispensable to us for discharging the duties of life. We cannot do without these two powers if we want to live like real men. And unless we cultivate them in childhood we cannot have them when we are grown up.

Our present system of education, however, does not allow us to cultivate them. We have to spend many years of our childhood in learning a foreign language taught by men not qualified for the job. To learn the English language is difficult enough, but to familiarize ourselves with English thought and feeling is even more difficult, and takes a long time during which our thinking capacity remains inactive for lack of an outlet . . .

When at last we manage to enter the realm of English ideas, we find that we are not quite at home there. We find that although we can somehow understand those ideas, we cannot absorb them into our deepest nature: that although we can use them in our lectures and writing we cannot use them in the practical affairs of our lives . . .

Education and life can never become one in such circumstances, and are bound to remain separated by a barrier. Our education may be compared to rainfall on a spot that is a long way from our roots. Not enough moisture seeps through the intervening barrier of earth to quench our thirst . . .

How to effect that union of education and life is today our most pressing problem. That union can be achieved only by Bengali language and literature.[19]

If we at all understand the needs of the present day, we must see that any new schools founded by us fulfil the following conditions: that their courses are both lively and varied, and nourish the heart as well as the intellect; that no disunity or discord disrupts the minds of our young; and that education does not become something unreal, heavy and abstract with which the pupils are concerned only for those few hours when they are at school.[20]

Brahmacharya gives power instead of mere instruction, and considers morality to be the essential ingredient, rather than the superficial ornament, of life. The person who practises it, far from regarding religion as something alien, takes to it easily and naturally as to a friend, and holds it close to his heart. It is not moral instruction that is needed for building up a boy's mind and character, but friendly guidance and congenial environment . . .

But nature's help is indispensable when we are still growing up, and still learning, and before we are drawn neck and crop into the whirlpool of affairs. Trees and rivers, and blue skies and beautiful views are just as necessary as benches and blackboards, books and examinations.[21]

If we had to build a school that would serve as a model, we should see that it was situated in a quiet spot far from the crowded city, and had the natural advantages of open sky, fields, trees and the like. It should be a retreat where teachers and students would live dedicated to learning.

If possible, there should be a plot of land which the students would help in cultivating, and which would provide food for the school. There should be cows for milk, and the students have a hand in tending them. When they are not engaged in study, the students should work in the garden, loosening the soil around the roots of trees, watering plants and training hedges. Their contact with natures would thus be both manual and mental.[22]

In education the most important factor is an atmosphere of creative activity, in which the work of intellectual exploration may find full scope . . . Further, our education should be in constant touch with our complete life, economic, intellectual, aesthetic, social and spiritual; and our schools should be at the very heart of our society, connected with it by the living bonds of varied co-operation.[23]

Let me state clearly that I have no distrust of any culture because of its foreign character. On the contrary, I believe that the shock of outside forces is necessary for maintaining the vitality of our intellect . . .

What I object to is the artificial arrangement by which this foreign education tends to occupy all the space of our national mind and thus kills, or hampers, the great opportunity for the creation of new thought by a combination of truths. It is this which makes me urge that all the elements in our own culture have to be strengthened, not to resist the culture of the West, but to accept and assimilate it. It must become for us nourishment and not a burden. We must gain mastery over it and not live on sufferance as hewers of texts and drawers of book-learning.[24]

I deeply hope that our educational centres will be the meeting ground of the East and the West. In the world of material gain human beings have neither stopped fighting, nor will they easily do so. But there are no obstacles to their meeting in the field of cultural exchange. The man who entertains no guests, living solely for himself, is petty-minded; that applies to a nation, too.[25]

I believe that the object of education is the freedom of the mind which can only be achieved through the path of freedom — though freedom has its risk and responsibility as life itself has. I know it for certain, though most people seem to have forgotten it, that children are living beings — more living than grown-up people, who have built their shells of habit around them. Therefore it is absolutely necessary for their mental health and development that they should not have mere schools for their lessons, but a world whose guiding spirit is personal love. It must be an *ashram* where men have gathered for the highest end of life, in the peace of nature . . .[26]

Hope

Tagore advocates the cultivation of hope rather than the passive acceptance of one's fate for the development of one's manhood.

It is not enough to say there is a shortage of funds in our country; worse, there is a shortage of hope. We cast all the blame on fate as we bear the torments of hunger. We grovel in the dust, assured that only the mercy of Heaven or of people from outside can save us. It does not strike us that the remedy is in our own hands.

That is why it is better to instil hope in the heart than to offer alms. It is his own deficiency, and no decree of fate, that makes a man sink into the depths. To think there is no escape from pre-ordained misery is to make the misery perpetual. To seek new paths in a constant renewal of strength — that has always been the secret of progress. When a man waits helplessly for a turning in the wheel of fortune, he has to be regarded as shorn of manhood.[27]

Politics

Self Government; Swarāj

The government in our country has no relationship with our society and no place in the social organization, so that, whatever we may seek from it must be bought at the expense of a certain freedom . . .

Today, of our own accord, we are ready to hand over to the government, one by one, the duties which had belonged to society. Many new communities appeared in our samaj in course of time and made special rules and conventions for themselves, while remaining within the Hindu fold; Hindu society never found fault with them. But everything is now tied down to the rigidity of the Englishman's law and any departure whatever is compelled to declare itself non-Hindu.[28]

Today a foreign king distributes titles among us as a reward for good deeds, but we shall truly be glorified only if we receive the benediction of our own countrymen. Unless we vest society with the power to give rewards, we shall deny ourselves a special satisfaction.[29]

Britain is bound to hold our souls in subjection until we forsake our inertness. To sit in a corner and bewail our losses will bear no fruit. To imitate the British and try to save ourselves by adopting a disguise is mere self-deception. We can never be real English-men, and we can never trick them by turning into imitation Englishmen.[30]

It is by exploiting our resources that the British have today become the leading power among nations. How can we expect that they will forgo easily what they hold? The conflict which faces us is no child's play and will need all our strength and all our patience. Anyone who adds to these difficulties by vain insolence and needless words is injuring the cause he professes to serve. We will accept fully the burdens of our task and refuse to admit defeat. We must free our industries, reshape our education and make the community strong and fit for service. It will need all our strength to do so and we shall strain every nerve in this stupen-dous endeavour . . .

Our aim must be to restore to the villages the power to meet their own requirements. We should combine a number of villages to form a regional unit. Self-government will become real only if the leaders of these units can make them self-reliant and capable of coping with the needs of their component villages. They must have their own schools, workshops and granaries, their own co-operative stores and banks which they should be assisted to found and taught to maintain. Each community unit should have its common meeting place for work and play where its appointed headmen may hear and settle local disputes and differences.[31]

When changes are introduced from outside, old social institu-tions fall into disuse and die. Nations that failed to evolve new institutions to meet the needs of a new age have disappeared in such crises of history. Shall we too be content to watch with listless eyes the slow extinction of our race? Malaria and famine and epidemic are not sudden visitations but symptoms of a chronic malady. Even more disturbing than these disasters is the deadly resignation that numbs our hearts. When a nation loses its self-confidence and no longer believes that it can do anything for itself, when a nation is content to submit to events as a decree of fate and beats it brow in helpless and hopeless passivity, it cannot withstand even a minor attack and the smallest scar becomes for it a fatal wound. A nation then invites death precisely because of its fear of death.[32]

Swaraj is not a matter of mere self-sufficiency in the production of cloth. Its real place is within us — the mind with its diverse power goes on building swaraj for itself. Nowhere in the world has this work been completed; in some part of the body-politic a lingering greed or delusion keeps up the bondage. And that bondage is always within the mind itself.

As everywhere else, swaraj in this country has to find its basis in the mind's unfoldment, in knowledge, in scientific thinking, and not in shallow gestures. It does not make sense to say that we could attain this swaraj by plying the spinning wheel a brief while.[33]

Swaraj for the whole of India would begin in the village where the people have formed themselves into a united community set on improving its health and education, its economic life, and its amusements no less. That swaraj would then advance by its own power, its propulsion inherent in the organic process of its own living growth, and not in the mechanical rotation of the spinning wheel.[34]

It is, I believe, essential that all over the country centres should be set up in which the responsibility for swaraj is accepted fully and not as a matter of homespun yarn alone. The people's welfare is an amalgam of several ingredients. To take one of them by itself cannot do much good. Health, recreation, the activities of the body and mind — thrown together in one combination, they make the picture complete . . .

The spread of co-operative self-determination in this concrete form, with its resultant inward experience of glory and pride, would be a solid foundation for swaraj.[35]

Economics

Boycott

We have been ordered to burn foreign cloth. I, for one am unable to obey. First, because I believe it to be my duty to fight the habit of blind obedience. Secondly, I feel that the cloth to be burned is not mine, it belongs to people who are sorely in need of it. We who seem to be doing an act of sacrifice through this incendiarism have other sources of supply; but those who are really hit cannot stir out of doors because of their nakedness. Forced atonement will not wash off our sins; nor will the gain of some apparent benefits make up for the loss of reasoned will.

The Mahatma has declared war against the tyranny of the machine which is oppressing the world. Here we are all under his banner. But we cannot accept as our ally in the fight the slave mentality that is at the root of all the misery and indignity in our national life. That, indeed, is our real enemy and through its defect alone can swaraj within and without come to us.

I am ready to burn cloth, but not under the blind pressure of a directive. Let experts give this question their time and thought and convince us with arguments what economic means could cure the economic malady arising from our use of foreign cloth. If we have committed an economic crime by using a certain make of cloth, how could we be sure, in the absence of logical data, that by burning cloth we would not simply broaden the basis of the crime, so that the stranglehold of Manchester would strengthen all the more?[36]

Machines

The factory may be an instrument of much wrong-doing, but it is not a thing that we can reject. The machine is also an organ of our vital force . . .

In the old days man applied his plough and loom, his bow and arrow, his wheeled vehicles, to the purpose of life's progress. So today should modern machines be made to serve the needs of humanity. It is true that because of the machine one rich man is served by thousands; but this only proves that one man can acquire the strength of thousands with the help of the machine. The power thus attained should not be monopolised by the few; it should be used for the benefit of the many. Let not power be concentrated to keep man apart. Let it never be irresponsible.[37]

Some say that, to avert disaster, the machines now employed by man should be scrapped. That is absurd. Quadrupeds have four feet but no arms. They somehow manage to do what is needed for a bare existence. This bare existence means poverty and defeat. Man, however, is fortunate in having been provided with two hands, which add vastly to his efficiency, an advantage that gives him mastery over all other living beings. When he increased his efficiency further, with the help of machines, he took one more step forward. It is absurd to suggest that this power of man should be curbed. Nations who have failed to gain control over the machine must face defeat, just as beasts had to face defeat from man.[38]

As the mills are killing our handicrafts, so is the all-pervading machinery of an alien government destroying our simple old village organizations. The results are invariably good when a small-scale unit expands with the increase in our demands, provided this is a natural development. The village organizations we had may have been small but they were essentially ours. What the British have set up may be grand but they do not belong to us. They not only make us passive but fail to satisfy our needs adequately. It will never do if we seek to use somebody else's eyes because we have lost our own.[39]

Wealth

Most of us who try to deal with the problem of poverty think only of a more intensive effort of production. We forget that it brings about a greater exhaustion of materials as well as of humanity. It gives to the few excessive opportunities for profit at the cost of the many. It is food which nourishes, not money; it is fullness of life which makes one happy, not fullness of purse. Multiplying material wealth alone intensifies the inequality between those who have and those who have not, and it inflicts so deep a wound on the social system that the whole body eventually bleeds to death.[40]

I do not believe that inequality in wealth can ever be completely removed by force. The disparity inherent in man is sure to assert itself. There is also the difference in temperament. Some love to hoard money while others have no inclination, so that unevenness in wealth is created. A mechanical uniformity is neither possible nor even desirable. As in the world of nature so in the world of man, complete uniformity paralizes initiative and makes the intellect idle. But excessive unevenness is equally bad, since it greatly hinders the development of social contact amongst people by the creation of distance between them. Evil builds its nest under the shadow of such barriers.[41]

Wealth acquired by a nation is meant to be shared with other nations, and a nation really deprives itself if it keeps all its wealth to itself. Science, nationhood, and democracy are the chief wealth of Europe, and the great tast of imparting it to India is the heaven-ordained royal mandate of British rule. We also have the task of reminding our rulers about that.[42]

Women

Men have seen the absurdity of today's civilization, which is based upon nationalism, — that is to say, on economics and politics and its consequent militarism. Men have been losing their freedom and their humanity in order to fit themselves for vast mechanical organisations. So the next civilization, it is hoped, will be based not merely upon economical and political competition and exploitation but upon world-wide social co-operation; upon spiritual ideals of reciprocity, and not upon economic ideals of efficiency. And then women will have their true place . . .

But woman can bring her fresh mind and all her power of sympathy to this new task of building up a spiritual civilization, if she will be conscious of her responsibilities.[43]

NOTES

1 Rabindranath Tagore, *The Religion of Man*, (London, 1970), 57 – 8.
2 Ibid., 71.
3 Ibid., 74.
4 Ibid., 89.
5 Ibid., 59 – 60.
6 Rabindranath Tagore, *Personality*, (London, 1921), 135.
7 Rabindranath Tagore, *Towards Universal Man*, (Bombay, 1961), 188.
8 *The Religion of Man*, 44.
9 Ibid., 11.
10 Ibid., 49.
11 Ibid., 102.
12 *Personality*, 27 – 8.
13 Rabindranath Tagore, *Gitanjali*, (London, 1926), 11.
14 *The Religion of Man*, 42 – 3.
15 *Personality*, 106.
16 Ibid., 67.
17 Ibid., 38.
18 *Gitanjali*, 29.
19 *Towards Universal Man*, 43 – 6.
20 Ibid., 68 – 9.
21 Ibid., 72.
22 Ibid., 75.
23 Ibid., 202 – 3.
24 Ibid., 222 – 3.
25 Ibid., 250.
26 *Personality*, 147 – 8.
27 *Towards Universal Man*, 323.

28 Ibid., 52 – 3.
29 Ibid., 60.
30 Ibid., 65.
31 Ibid., 118 – 9.
32 Ibid., 122.
33 Ibid., 268.
34 Ibid., 284.
35 Ibid., 282 – 3.
36 Ibid., 269 – 70.
37 Ibid., 306 – 7.
38 Ibid., 334 – 5.
39 Ibid., 121.
40 Ibid., 316.
41 Ibid., 339.
42 Ibid., 197 – 8.
43 *Personality*, 183.

REFERENCES

Rabindranath Tagore, *The Religion of Man*. London: Unwin Books, 1970.
Rabindranath Tagore, *Personality: Lectures Delivered in America*. London: Macmillan, 1921.
Rabindranath Tagore, *Towards Universal Man*. Bombay: Asia Publishing House, 1961.
Rabindranath Tagore, *Gitanjali (Song Offerings)*. London, Macmillan, 1926.

11

MOHANDĀS KARAMCHAND GANDHI (1869 – 1948)

Born in Porbandar, Gujarat in 1869, the youngest son of Kaba
Gandhi and his fourth wife Putlibai, both members of the Bania
caste, Gandhi refers to his father as truthful, incorruptible, brave,
generous but short-tempered and his mother as saintly and deeply
religious. The influence of his home and Hindu upbringing
remained with him throughout his life to inform his teaching and
determine the spirit in which he lived. He is faithful to the traditions of Hinduism when he affirms the isomorphism of Truth
(*Satya*) and Reality (*Sat*) and it is not without significance that he
subtitles his autobiography 'The Story of My Experiments with
Truth'. His whole life might well be interpreted as an attempt to
live in accordance with, and as an existential quest for, Truth.

His early marriage at the age of thirteen to Kasturbai convinced
him of the folly of the custom of child marriages in Hindu society
and he regarded his enforced separations from his wife and infant
son after five years, when he left for England to study law, as a
beneficial event for both of them. Experiments in meat-eating
which he had engaged in with school friends in India, contrary to
the Vaishnava faith which the Gandhis upheld and the view of the
Jains who were influential in Gujarat, were resisted in England
despite the constant entreaty of friends. The vow he made to his
mother to abstain from meat-eating was vindicated when the
benefits of vegetarianism were made clear to him from literature
he read on the subject.

Contact with theosophists in England introduced him to Sir
Edwin Arnold's translation of the Bhagavad Gītā, *The Song
Celestial*, which made a deep impression on him, and *The Light of
Asia*, which together with Madame Blavatsky's *Key to Theology*,
stimulated in him the desire to learn more about his native
Hinduism. He realized his purpose in going to England when he
was called to the bar on 10 June 1891; two days later he sailed for
India.

His attempt to practise law first in Bombay and then Rajkot
met with limited success so when he was offered a court case in
South Africa relating to Abdulla Sheth, a Muslim merchant, he
accepted. Soon after his arrival in Natal he travelled to Durban on
a first-class train ticket, but at Maritzburg he was forcibly ejected

from the train when he refused to vacate the first-class compartment reserved for whites. He regarded this experience, and other hardships he encountered, as symptomatic of the disease of colour prejudice in South Africa which he resolved to try to root out. In the pursuit of this aim, he founded the Natal Indian Congress which publicized the general condition of Natal Indians including their disenfranchised state.

His period in South Africa was formative in that it enhanced his regard for Hinduism and made him aware of the interrelation of self-realization, the realization of God and the service of others. His awareness, strengthened by the influence of Ruskin's *Unto This Last*, eventually took the form of the equation of *Satya*, Truth or God, and *Sat*, Being, with *Ātman*, the highest self, and the acceptance of *sarvodaya*, the welfare of all men, together with the unitary nature of existence, as the natural corollary of Truth. The unity of all life he saw as the basis of *ahiṁsā* or non-violence, since injury to one could not but affect all. This led him in time to stress the interrelation of *ahiṁsā* and Truth.

The implementation of *ahiṁsā* took the form of *satyāgraha*, a word first coined by Gandhi in South Africa to express the desire to hold firm to Truth, and one which gave practical expression to the religious and ethical ideals of Truth and non-violence. His decision, with the consent of his wife, to take the *brahmacārya* vow, the vow of chastity, is linked to the self-discipline and dedication required of satyāgrahis and indicative of his determination to devote himself to the realization of Truth through the service of others. Satyāgraha was successfully applied against the Asiatic Registration Act of the Transvaal Government which required every Indian to take out a certificate of registration and to produce it on demand. It was implemented successfully in India in the case of the peasant cultivators of Kheda who sought suspension of the payment of an annual revenue assessment because of the failure of crops and an impending famine; on behalf of the untouchables who were forbidden to use the roads in the vicinity of the Vykom temple in Travancore; against the British indigo planters at Champaran where ryots were being unfairly treated; and in the dispute between textile mill-owners and labourers in Ahmedabad where Gandhi first fasted as a self-imposed form of suffering.

Gandhi's belief in the absolute oneness of God and humanity and the interrelation of Truth, *ahiṁsā, satyāgraha* and *sarvodaya* had far-reaching social, economic and political implications. It determined his attitude to the untouchables whom he significantly called Harijans, children of God; towards women, whose status in traditional Hindu society was far from enviable; towards education where, in his view, equality of opportunity should prevail; and towards *Swarāj*, or self-rule, which for him was grounded in Truth and the undisputed right of the people of India.

His assassination at the hands of the young Hindu fanatic Nathuram Godse ended the life of one of the most remarkable men of this century. He rejected the title of saint as being too sacred a term to be applied to a simple seeker after truth, but there can be no doubt that he was India's Mahātma, Great Soul.

MOHANDĀS KARAMCHAND GANDHI

Truth and God

If I had only to discuss academic principles, I should clearly not attempt an autobiography. But my purpose being to give an account of various practical applications of these principles, I have given the chapters I propose to write the title of *The Story of My Experiments with Truth*. These will of course include experiments with non-violence, celibacy and other principles of conduct believed to be distinct from truth. But for me, truth is the sovereign principle, which includes numerous other principles. This truth is not only truthfulness in word, but truthfulness in thought also, and not only the relative truth of our conception, but the Absolute Truth, the Eternal Principle, that is God . . . But I worship God as Truth only. I have not yet found Him, but I am seeking after Him . . . But as long as I have not realized this Absolute Truth, so long must I hold by the relative truth as I have conceived it. That relative truth must, meanwhile, be my beacon, my shield and buckler . . . Even my Himalayan blunders have seemed trifling to me because I have kept strictly to this path. For the path has saved me from coming to grief, and I have gone forward according to my light. Often in my progress I have had faint glimpses of the Absolute Truth, God, and daily the conviction is growing upon me that He alone is real and all else is unreal.[1]

My uniform experience has convinced me that there is no other God than truth . . . The little fleeting glimpses, therefore, that I have been able to have of Truth can hardly convey an idea of the indescribable lustre of Truth, a million times more intense than that of the sun we daily see with our eyes . . . But this much I can say with assurance, as a result of all my experiments, that a perfect vision of Truth can only follow a complete realization of *Ahimsa*.

To see the universal and all-pervading Spirit of Truth face to face one must be able to love the meanest of creation as oneself. And a man who aspires after that cannot afford to keep out of any field of life. That is why my devotion to Truth has drawn me into the field of politics.[2]

The word *Satya* (Truth) is derived from *Sat*, which means 'being'. Nothing is or exists in reality except Truth. That is why *Sat* or Truth is perhaps the most important name of God. In fact it is more correct to say that Truth is God, than to say that God is Truth . . .

It is That which alone is, which constitutes the stuff of which all things are made, which subsists by virtue of its own power, which is not supported by anything else but supports everything that exists. Truth alone is eternal, everything else is momentary.[3]

And when you want to find Truth as God the only inevitable means is Love, i.e., non-violence, and since I believe that ultimately the means and end are convertible terms, I should not hesitate to say that God is Love . . .

God is not a person . . . The truth is that God is the force. He is the essence of life. He is pure and undefiled consciousness. He is eternal . . .

God is not some person outside ourselves or away from the universe. He pervades everything, and is omniscient as well as omnipotent. He does not need any praise or petitions. Being imminent in all beings, He hears everything and reads our innermost thoughts. He abides in our hearts and is nearer to us than the nails are to the fingers.[4]

Truth has no form. Therefore everyone will form such an idea or image of truth as appeals to him, and there will be as many images of truth as there are men.[5]

Ahimsa and Truth are so intertwined that it is practically impossible to disentangle and separate them. They are like the two sides of an coin, or rather a smooth unstamped metallic disc. Who can say, which is the obverse, and which the reverse? Nevertheless, *ahimsa* is the means; Truth is the end.[6]

God is that indefinable something which we all feel but which we do not know. To me God is Truth and Love, God is ethics and morality. God is fearlessness, God is the source of light and life and yet He is above and beyond all these. God is consciousness. He is even the atheism of the atheist. He transcends speech and reason. He is a personal God to those who need His touch. He is the purest essence. He simply Is to those who have faith.[7]

I do not regard God as a person. Truth for me is God, and God's Law and God are not different things or facts, in the sense that an earthly king and his law are different.[8]

But it is not impossible for me to realize perfect Truth so long as we are imprisoned in this mortal frame. We can only visualize it in our imagination. We cannot, through the instrumentality of this ephemeral body, see face to face Truth which is eternal. That is why in the last resort one must depend on faith.[9]

What I want to achieve — what I have been striving and pining to achieve these thirty years — is self-realization, to see God face to face, to attain *Moksha*.[10]

Religion

Let me explain what I mean by religion. It is not the Hindu religion which I certainly prize above all other religions, but the *religion* which transcends Hinduism, which changes one's very nature, which binds one indissolubly to the truth within and which ever purifies. It is the permanent element in human nature which counts no cost too great in order to find full expression and which leaves the soul utterly restless until it has found itself, known its Maker and appreciated the true correspondence between the Maker and itself.[11]

True religion and true morality are inseparably bound up with each other. Religion is to morality what water is to the seed that is sown in the soil.[12]

Indeed religion should pervade every one of our actions. Here religion does not mean sectarianism. It means a belief in ordered moral government of the universe. It is not less real because it is unseen. This religion transcends Hinduism, Islam, Christianity, etc. It does not supersede them. It harmonizes them and gives them reality.[13]

Religions are different roads converging to the same point. What does it matter that we take different roads, so long as we reach the same goal? In reality there are as many religions as there are individuals.[14]

So long as there are different religions, every one of them may need some distinctive symbol. But when the symbol is made into a fetish and an instrument of proving the superiority of one's religion over other's it is fit only to be discarded.[15]

We have not realised religion in its perfection, even as we have not realised God. Religion of our conception, being thus imperfect, is always subject to a process of evolution and reinterpretation . . .

Even as a tree has a single trunk, but many branches and leaves, so there is one true and perfect Religion, but it becomes many, as it passes through the human medium. The one Religion is beyond all speech.[16]

Religion does not teach us to bear ill-will towards one another. It is easy enough to be friendly to one's friends. But to befriend the one who regards himself as your enemy, is the quintessence of true religion.[17]

After long study and experience, I have come to the conclusion that (1) all religions are true; (2) all religions have some error in them; (3) all religions are almost as dear to me as my own Hinduism, in as much as all human beings should be as dear to one as one's own close relatives. My own veneration for other faiths is the same as that for my own faith; therefore no thought of conversion is possible.[18]

Let no one even for a moment entertain the fear that a reverent study of other religions is likely to weaken or shake one's faith in one's own. The Hindu system of philosophy regards all religions as containing the elements of truth in them and enjoins an attitude of respect and reverence towards them all.[19]

As soon as we lose the moral basis, we cease to be religious. There is no such thing as religion overriding morality. Man for instance cannot be untruthful, cruel and incontinent and claim to have God on his side.[20]

The acceptance of the doctrine of Equality of Religions does not abolish the distinction between religion and irreligion. We do not propose to cultivate toleration for irreligion.[21]

I believe in the fundamental truth of all great religions of the world. I believe that they are all God-given, and I believe that they were necessary for the people to whom these religions were revealed. And I believe that, if only we could all of us read the scriptures of different faiths from the standpoint of the followers of those faiths we should find that they were at bottom all one and were all helpful to one another.[22]

Ahiṁsā and Satyāgraha

Ahimsa means 'Love' in the Pauline sense, and yet something more than the 'Love' defined by St Paul, although I know St Paul's beautiful definition is good enough for all practical purposes. *Ahimsa* includes the whole creation, and not only human
. . .
Ahimsa is not merely a negative state of harmlessness, but it is a positive state of love, of doing good even to the evil-doer. But it

does not mean helping the evil-doer to continue the wrong or tolerating it by passive acquiescence. On the contrary, love — the active state of *Ahimsa* — requires you to resist the wrong-doer by dissociating yourself from him, even though it may offend him or injure him physically . . .

It is no non-violence if we merely love those that love us. It is non-violence only when we love those that hate us . . .

Ahimsa is an attribute of the brave. Cowardice and *Ahimsa* do not go together any more than water and fire.[23]

Ahimsa is a comprehensive principle. We are helpless mortals caught in the conflagration of *himsa*. The saying that life lives on life has a deep meaning in it. Man cannot for a moment live without consciously or unconsciously committing outward *himsa*. The very fact of his living — eating, drinking and moving about — necessarily involves some *himsa*, destruction of life, be it ever so minute. A votary of *ahimsa* therefore remains true to his faith if the spring of all his actions is compassion, if he shuns to the best of his ability the destruction of the tiniest creature, tries to save it, and thus incessantly strives to be free from the deadly coil of *himsa*.[24]

Satyagraha is soul force pure and simple, and whenever and to whatever extent there is room for the use of arms or physical force or brute force, there and to that extent is there so much less possibility for soul force. These are purely antagonistic forces in my view, and I had full realization of this antagonism even at the time of the advent of Satyagraha.[25]

Satyagraha differs from Passive Resistance as the North Pole from the South. The latter has been conceived as a weapon of the weak and does not exclude the use of physical force or violence for the purpose of gaining one's end, whereas the former has been conceived as a weapon of the strongest and excludes the use of violence in any shape or form.

The term *Satyagraha* was coined by me in South Africa to express the force that the Indians there used for full eight years and it was coined in order to distinguish it from the movement then going on in the United Kingdom and South Africa under the name of Passive Resistance.

Its root meaning is holding on to truth, hence Truth-force. I have also called it Love-force or Soul-force. In the application of *Satyagraha* I have discovered in the earliest stages that pursuit of truth did not admit of violence being inflicted on one's opponent but that he must be weaned from error by patience and sympathy.

For what appears to be truth to the one may appear to be error to the other. And patience means self-suffering. So the doctrine came to mean vindication of Truth not by infliction of suffering on the opponent but on one's self.[26]

Satyagraha is a relentless search for truth and a determination to reach the truth . . .

There can be no *Satyagraha* in an unjust cause. *Satyagraha* in a just cause is vain, if the men espousing it are not determined and capable of fighting and suffering to the end, and the slightest use of violence often defeats a just cause. *Satyagraha* excludes the use of violence in any shape or form, whether in thought, speech, or deed. Given a just cause, capacity for endless suffering and avoidance of violence, victory is a certainty . . .

Satyagraha is gentle, it never wounds. It must not be the result of anger or malice. It is never fussy, never impatient, never vociferous. It is the direct opposite of compulsion. It was conceived as a complete substitute for violence.[27]

Non-cooperation and civil disobedience are but different branches of the same tree called *Satyagraha* . . .

Every *Satyagrahi* was bound to resist all those laws which he considered to be unjust and which were not of a criminal character, in order to bend the Government to the will of the people.[28]

Civil disobedience therefore becomes a sacred duty when the state has become lawless, or which is the same thing, corrupt. And a citizen that barters with such a State shares its corruptness or lawlessness.[29]

Fasting unto death is the last and the most potent weapon in the armoury of *Satyagraha*. It is a sacred thing. But it must be accepted with all its implications. It is not the fast itself, but what it implies that matters.[30]

Of course it is not to be denied that fasts can be really coercive. Such are fasts to attain a selfish object . . . I would unhesitatingly advocate resistance of such undue influence . . . And if it is argued that the dividing line between a selfish and unselfish end is often very thin, I would urge that a person who regards the end of a fast to be selfish or otherwise base should resolutely refuse to yield to it, even though the refusal may result in the death of the fasting person.[31]

My fast was undertaken not on account of the lapse of the mill-owners, but on account of that of the labourers in which, as their representative, I felt I had a share. With the mill-owners, I could only plead; to fast against them would amount to coercion. Yet in spite of my knowledge that my fast was bound to put pressure upon them, as in fact it did, I felt I could not help it. The duty to undertake it seemed to me to be clear.[32]

Sarvodaya: Untouchability and Women

I do not believe in the doctrine of the greatest good of the greatest number. It means in its nakedness that in order to achieve the supposed good of fifty-one per cent, the interest of forty-nine per cent may be, or rather, should be sacrificed. It is a heartless doctrine and has done harm to humanity. The only real, dignified, human doctrine is the greatest good of all, and this can only be achieved by uttermost self-sacrifice.[33]

A votary of *ahimsa* cannot subscribe to the utilitarian formula (of the greatest good of the greatest number). He will strive for the greatest good of all and die in the attempt to realize the ideal. He will therefore be willing to die, so that the others may live. He will serve himself with the rest, by himself dying . . . The utilitarian to be logical will never sacrifice himself. The absolutist will even sacrifice himself.[34]

I believe in absolute oneness of God and therefore also of humanity. What though we have many bodies? We have but one soul. The rays of the sun are many through refraction. But they have the same source.[35]

I do not believe that an individual may gain spiritually and those that surround him suffer. I believe in *advaita*. I believe in the essential unity of man and for that matter of all that lives.[36]

I believe that every man is born in the world with certain natural tendencies. Every person is born with certain definite limitations which he cannot overcome. From a careful observation of those limitations the law of *varna* was deduced.[37]

Varnashrama of the *shastras* is today non-existent in practice. The present caste system is the very antithesis of *varnashrama*. The sooner public opinion abolishes it the better.[38]

Caste has nothing to do with religion. It is harmful both to spiritual and national growth.[39]

Hinduism has sinned in giving sanction to untouchability. It has degraded us, made us *pariahs*. Even the Mussalmans have caught the sinful contagion from us.[40]

The 'touch-me-not'-ism that disfigures the present-day Hinduism is a morbid growth. It only betrays a woodenness of mind, a blind self-conceit. It is abhorrent alike to the spirit of religion and morality.[41]

I do not want to be reborn. But if I have to be reborn, I should be born an untouchable, so that I may share their sorrows, sufferings, and affronts levelled at them, in order that I may endeavour to free myself and them from that miserable condition.[42]

None can be born untouchable, as all are sparks of one and the same Fire. It is wrong to treat certain human beings as untouchables from birth . . .
Removal of untouchability means love for, and service of, the whole world, and thus merges into *ahimsa*. Removal of untouchability spells the breaking down of barriers between man and man, and between the various orders of Being.[43]

I think we are committing a great sin in treating a whole class of people as untouchables and it is owing to the existence of this class that we have still some revolting practices among us . . .
It has been a passion of my life to serve the untouchables because I have felt that I could not remain a Hindu if it was true that untouchability was a part of Hinduism.[44]

Of all the evils for which man has made himself responsible, none to me, is so degrading, so shocking or so brutal as his abuse of the better half of humanity, the female sex, not the weaker sex. It is the nobler of the two, for it is even today the embodiment of sacrifice, silent suffering, humility, faith and knowledge.[45]

Man should learn to give place to women and a community or country in which women are not honoured cannot be considered as civilized . . .
Chastity is not a hot-house growth. It cannot be superimposed. It cannot be protected by the surrounding wall of the *purdah*. It must grow from within, and to be worth anything, it must be capable of withstanding every unsought temptation.[46]

Marriage must cease to be a matter of arrangement made by parents for money. The system is ultimately connected with caste. So long as the choice is restricted to a few hundred young men or women of a particular caste, the system will persist no matter what is said against it. The girls or boys or their parents will have to break the bonds of caste if the evil is to be eradicated. All this means education of a character that will revolutionize the mentality of the youth of the nation.[47]

If we would be pure, if we would save Hinduism, we must rid ourselves of this poison of enforced widowhood. The reform must begin by those who have girl-widows taking courage in both their hands and seeing that the child-widows in their charge are duly and well married — not remarried. They were never really married.[48]

The least that a parent, who has so abused his trust as to give in marriage an infant to an old man in his dotage or to a boy hardly in his teens, can do, is to purge himself of his sin by remarrying his daughter when she becomes widowed. As I have said in a previous note, such marriages should be declared null and void from the beginning.[49]

Education

By education I mean an all-round drawing out of the best in child and man — body, mind and spirit. Literacy is not the end of education nor even the beginning. It is only one of the means whereby man and woman can be educated. Literacy in itself is no education. I would therefore begin the child's education by teaching it a useful handicraft and enabling it to produce from the moment it begins its training.[50]

My plan to impart primary education through the medium of village handicrafts like spinning and carding, etc., is thus conceived as the spearhead of a silent revolution fraught with the most far-reaching consequences. It will provide a healthy and moral basis of relationship between the city and the village and thus go a long way towards eradicating some of the worst evils of the present social insecurity and poisoned relationship between the classes. It will check the progressive decay of our villages and lay the foundation of a juster social order in which there is no unnatural division between the 'haves' and 'have-nots' and everybody is assured of a living wage and the right to freedom.[51]

A curriculum of religious education should include a study of the tenets of faiths other than one's own. For this purpose the students should be trained to cultivate the habit of understanding and appreciating the doctrines of various great religions of the world in a spirit of reverence and broad-minded tolerance.[52]

The suggestion has often been made that in order to make education compulsory, or even available to every boy or girl wishing to receive education, our schools and colleges should

become almost, if not wholly, self-supporting, not through dona-
tions or State aid or fees exacted from students, but through
remunerative work done by the students themselves. This can only
be done by making industrial training compulsory . . .

It is impossible to exaggerate the harm we do to India's youth
by filling their minds with the false notion that it is ungentlemanly
to labour with one's hands and feet for one's livelihood or schooling.[53]

The aim of university education should be to turn out true servants of the people who will live and die for the country's
freedom. I am therefore of the opinion that university education
should be co-ordinated and brought into line with basic education.[54]

In my opinion it is not for a democratic State to find money for
founding universities. If the people want them they will supply the
funds. Universities so founded will adorn the country which they
represent.[55]

The school must be an extension of home; there must be concordance between the impressions which a child gathers at home
and at school, — if the best results are to be obtained. Education
through the medium of a strange tongue breaks the concordance
which should exist. Those who break this relationship are the
enemies of the people even though their motives may be honest.[56]

Among the many evils of foreign rule, this blighting imposition
of a foreign medium upon the youth of the country will be
counted by history as one of the greatest. It has sapped the energy
of the nation, it has shortened the lives of the pupils. It has
estranged them from the masses, it has made education unnecessarily expensive. If this process is still persisted in, it bids fair to
rob the nation of its soul. The sooner, therefore, educated India
shakes itself free from the hypnotic spell of the foreign medium,
the better it would be for them and the people.[57]

In my opinion the existing system of education is defective,
apart from its association with an utterly unjust Government, in
three most important matters:
(1) It is based on foreign culture to the almost entire exclusion of
    indigenous culture.
(2) It ignores the culture of the heart and the hand, and confines
    itself simply to the head.
(3) Real education is impossible through a foreign medium.[58]

The medium of a foreign language through which higher education has been imparted in India has caused incalculable intellectual and moral injury to the nation. We are too near our own
times to judge the enormity of the damage done. And we who
have received such education have both to be victims and judges
— an almost impossible feat.[59]

I do not want my house to be walled in on all sides and my win-
dows to be stuffed. I want the cultures of all lands to be blown
about my house as freely as possible. But I refuse to be blown off
my feet by any. I would have our young men and women with
literary tastes to learn as much of English and other world-
languages as they like, and then expect them to give the benefits of
their learning to India and to the world like a Bose, a Roy or the
Poet himself. But I would not have a single Indian to forget,
neglect or be ashamed of his mother tongue, or to feel that he or
she cannot think or express the best thoughts in his or her own
vernacular. Mine is not a religion of the prison-house.[60]

Politics and Economics

Dignity of Labour

You must teach the people to labour with their hands and realize
the dignity of work.[61]

My *Ahimsa* would not tolerate the idea of giving a free meal to
a healthy person who has not worked for it in some honest way,
and if I had the power, I would stop every *Sadavrata* where free
meals are given. It has degraded the nation and it has encouraged
laziness, idleness, hypocrisy and even crime.[62]

Swadeshī

Swadeshi is that spirit in us which restricts us to the use of the service of our immediate surroundings to the exclusion of the more
remote . . . In the domain of politics, I should make use of the
indigenous institutions and serve them by curing them of their
proved defects. In that of economics I should use only things that
are produced by my immediate neighbours and serve those industries by making them efficient and complete where they might
be found wanting.[63]

Trusteeship

My idea of society is that while we are born equal, meaning that
we have a right to equal opportunity, all have not the same capacity. It is, in the nature of things, impossible . . .

I am inviting those people who consider themselves owners
today to act as trustees, e.g., owners, not in their own right, but
owners, in the right of those whom they have exploited.[64]

Trusteeship provides a means of transforming the present
capitalist order of society into an egalitarian one. It gives no
quarter to capitalism, but gives the present owning class a chance
of reforming itself. It is based on the faith that human nature is
never beyond redemption.[65]

If they (capitalists) proved impervious to the appeal of reason,
the weapon of non-violent non-cooperation would be brought
into play.[66]

Industrialization

Pauperism must go. But industrialism is no remedy. The evil does
not lie in the use of bullock carts. It lies in our selfishness and
want of consideration for our neighbours. If we have not love for
our neighbours, no change however revolutionary, can do us any
good.[67]

Machinery has its place; it has come to stay. But it must not be
allowed to displace the necessary human labour . . .

That use of machinery is lawful which subserves the interest of
all . . .

I would favour the use of the most elaborate machinery if
thereby India's pauperism and resulting idleness be avoided. I
have suggested hand-spinning as the only ready means of driving
away penury and making famine of work and wealth impossible.
The spinning-wheel itself is a piece of valuable machinery, and in
my own humble way I have tried to secure improvements in it in
keeping with the special condition of India . . .

What I object to, is the *craze* for machinery not machinery as
such. The craze is for what they call labour-saving machinery.
Men go on 'saving labour', till thousands are without work and
thrown on the open streets to die of starvation.[68]

Khādī

Khadi connotes the beginning of economic freedom and equality of all in the country . . . It means wholesale *Swadeshi* mentality, a determination to find all the necessaries of life in India and that too through the labour and intellect of the villagers.[69]

When once we have revived the one industry (*Khadi*), all the other industries will follow. I would make the spinning wheel the foundation on which to build a sound village life; I would make the wheel the centre round which all other activities will revolve.[70]

Khadi is the sun of the village solar system. The planets are the various industries which can support *Khadi* in return for the heat and the sustenance they derive from it. Without it, the other industries cannot grow.[71]

Swarāj

The word *Swaraj* is a sacred word, a Vedic word, meaning self-rule and self-restraint, and not freedom from all restraint which 'independence' often means.[72]

As every country is fit to eat, to drink and to breathe, even so is every nation fit to manage its own affairs, no matter how badly.[73]

Self-government depends entirely upon our internal strength, upon our ability to fight against the heaviest odds. Indeed, self-government which does not require that continuous striving to attain it and to sustain it is not worth the name. I have, therefore, endeavoured to show both in word and deed, that political self-government, that is, self-government for a large number of men and women, is no better than individual self-government, and, therefore, it is to be attained by precisely the same means that are required for individual self-government or self-rule.[74]

Swaraj for me means freedom for the meanest of our country-men . . . I am not interested in freeing India merely from the English yoke. I am bent upon freeing India from any yoke what-soever.[75]

Nationalism

Our nationalism can be no peril to other nations, inasmuch as we will exploit none just as we will allow none to exploit us. Through *Swaraj* we would serve the whole world.[76]

My love, therefore, of nationalism or my idea of nationalism is that my country may become free, that if need be the whole of the country may die, so that the human race may live. There is not room for race hatred there. Let that be our nationalism.[77]

My patriotism is not an exclusive thing. It is all-embracing and I should reject that patriotism which sought to mount upon the distress or the exploitation of other nationalities. The conception of my patriotism is nothing if it is not always in every case without exception consistent with the broadest good of humanity at large.[78]

We want freedom for our country, but not at the expense or exploitation of others, not so as to degrade other countries. I do not want the freedom of India if it means the extinction of England or the disappearance of Englishmen. I want the freedom of my country so that other countries may learn something from my free country, so that the resources of my country might be utilized for the benefit of mankind.[79]

NOTES

1 *Selected Works*, I, xxi.
2 Ibid., II, 752 – 3.
3 *The Selected Works*, Vol VI, 96.
4 Ibid., 100 – 1.
5 Ibid., Vol V, 382 – 3.
6 *Selections from Gandhi*, 13.
7 Ibid., 3.
8 Ibid., 6.
9 Ibid., 8.
10 *Selected Works*, I, xix.
11 *Selections*, 254; cf. *Selected Works*, VI, 263.
12 *Selections*, 255.
13 Ibid., 256.
14 Ibid.
15 Ibid.
16 *Selected Works*, IV, 240 – 2; cf. *Selections*, 257.

17 *Selections*, 258.
18 Ibid., 258; cf. *Selected Works*, 269.
19 *Selections*, 258.
20 Ibid., 255.
21 Ibid., 244.
22 *Selected Works*, VI, 264.
23 Ibid., 153 – 6.
24 Ibid., II, 521 – 2.
25 *Selected Works*, III, 155.
26 *Selected Works*, VI, 179.
27 Ibid., 185 – 7.
28 Ibid., 209.
29 Ibid., 212.
30 Ibid., 216.
31 Ibid., 217.
32 On the occasion of the strike of mill-hands at Ahmedabad, ibid., II, 644.
33 *Selected Works*, VI, 230 – 1.
34 Ibid., 230.
35 *Selections*, 25.
36 Ibid.
37 Ibid., 265.
38 Ibid.
39 Ibid.
40 Ibid., 268.
41 Ibid., 268 – 9.
42 Ibid., 269.
43 *Selected Works*, IV, 235, 237.
44 *Selected Works*, V, 443.
45 Ibid., VI, 486.
46 Ibid., 489.
47 Ibid., 494.
48 Ibid., 494 – 5.
49 *Selections*, 274.
50 *Selected Works*, VI, 507.
51 Ibid., 512.
52 Ibid., 519.
53 Ibid., 519 – 20.
54 Ibid., 521.
55 Ibid., 523.
56 Ibid., 526.
57 Ibid., 528.
58 *Selections*, 283.
59 Ibid., 293.
60 Ibid., 298.
61 *Selected Works*, IV, 330.
62 Ibid., 334.
63 Ibid., 336.
64 Ibid., 366.
65 Ibid., 373.
66 Ibid., 375.
67 Ibid., 376.
68 Ibid., 379 – 80.

69 Ibid., 385.
70 Ibid., 393.
71 Ibid., 398.
72 Ibid., 440.
73 Ibid.
74 Ibid., 440 – 1.
75 Ibid., 442.
76 Ibid., 247.
77 Ibid., 248.
78 Ibid., 247.
79 *Selections*, 42.

REFERENCES

The Selected Works of Mahatma Gandhi. Ahmedabad: Navajivan Publishing
House, 1969, Vols I – VI.
Nimal Kumar Bose, *Selections from Gandhi*, Ahmedabad: Navajivan Publishing
House, 1948, 1972.

12

AUROBINDO GHOSE (1872 – 1950)

Aurobindo was born in Konnagar in West Bengal into an influential family with close connections with the Brahmo Samāj. His father was an anglophile with a passion for all things Western and he arranged for his children to be educated in European schools in India and then in England. Aurobindo's schooling began at the Loretto Convent, Darjeeling, and from the age of seven at a preparatory school in England before entering St Paul's School, London. A classical scholarship took him to King's College, Cambridge, where he proved himself a successful student. He returned to India in 1893 and entered the civil service of the state of Baroda. He was thoroughly trained in Western thought but had only a rudimentary knowledge of Indian literature and philosophy. This deficiency he sought to remedy by devoting himself to the study of the cultural heritage of India for a period of years until his sympathies led him inevitably into the maelstrom of Bengal politics.

For a time Aurobindo was a popular political leader and a close associate of Tilak. He acquired a reputation for being a remarkable orator and his journalistic articles were so inflammatory that he was accused by the government of sedition, a charge that was never proven. His political activities, however, eventually led to his being charged with advocating terrorism and violence. He was arrested and jailed at Alipur in 1908 and during his period of incarceration became attracted to the pursuit of spiritual ideals. After his release he spent a few months at Chandernagore near Calcutta and then, in 1910, withdrew to the French settlement of Pondicherry where he remained for forty years engaged in writing. His philosophical system of integral yoga is the fruit of those forty years of study and contemplation.

Aurobindo is generally accepted as one of the foremost mystical philosophers of India. The essence of his philosophical system, which he describes as Vedāntic, is that the Absolute by a process of involution and evolution manifests itself in, and expresses itself through, grades of reality or levels of being from matter to spirit. The Absolute is the starting point of the evolutionary ascent from lower forms of matter through mind to supermind and spirit and the involutionary descent of the spirit through supermind to mind and matter. For Aurobindo every aspect of reality is permeated by the Absolute and the veil between mind and supermind is where the higher and lower levels of reality meet. The rending of the veil by involution and evolution is the prerequisite of the development of divine consciousness and divine life within humanity. This divine life might be character- ized as gnostic being; it is a life that participates in the power, sovereignty and infinitude of the Absolute and manifests the fullness of spirituality. To know and realize the Absolute as Saccidānanda, as one in itself and in all its manifestations, is the essence and goal of integral yoga. It is also the achievement of gnostic beings who, because of their spirituality and cosmic con- sciousness, are capable of effecting the transformation of lower levels of being and the whole nature. Not for Aurobindo the circumscribed goal of individual liberation. He aims at the total transformation of man and nature. He seeks the reconciliation of matter and mind, mind and spirit, finite and infinite, God and man. His philosophy is a philosophy of synthesis.

Aurobindo's attempt at reconciliation and synthesis extended to Eastern and Western philosophy. It involved him in the use of both Hindu and Western modes of thought and his complex system is marked by spiritual insights expressed in highly esoteric terminology. Though he failed to stir the imagination of the people in the same way as men like Vivekānanda and Gandhi he still succeeded in inspiring enthusiasm in small groups of intellec- tuals for the cultural heritage of India, especially the Vedas and the Upanishads in which his philosophy is firmly rooted.

AUROBINDO GHOSE

Religion

Involution and Evolution

This Divine Being, Sachchidananda, is at once impersonal and personal: it is an Existence and the origin and foundation of all truths, forces, powers, existences, but is also the one transcendent Conscious Being and the All-Person of whom all conscious beings are the selves and personalities; for He is their highest Self and the universal indwelling Presence . . .

The manifestation of the Being in our universe takes the shape of an involution which is the starting-point of an evolution, — Matter the nethermost stage, Spirit the summit.[1]

An involution of the Divine Existence, the spiritual Reality, in the apparent inconscience of Matter is the starting-point of the evolution. But that Reality is in its nature an eternal Existence, Consciousness, Delight of Existence: the evolution must then be an emergence of this Existence, Consciousness, Delight of Existence, not at first in its essence or totality but in evolutionary forms that express or diagnose it.[2]

An original creative or evolutionary Power there must be: but, although Matter is the first substance, the original and ultimate Power is not an inconscient material Energy; for then life and consciousness would be absent, since Inconscience cannot evolve consciousness nor an inanimate Force evolve life. There must be, therefore, since Mind and Life also are not that, a secret Consciousness greater than Life — Consciousness or Mind-Consciousness, an Energy more essential than the material Energy. Since it is greater than Mind, it must be supramental Consciousness — Force; since it is a power of essential substance other than Matter, it must be the power of that which is the supreme essence and substance of all things, a power of the Spirit.[3]

If a spiritual unfolding on earth is the hidden truth of our birth into Matter, if it is fundamentally an evolution of consciousness that has been taking place in Nature, then man as he is cannot be the last term of that evolution: he is too imperfect an expression of the Spirit, Mind itself a too limited form and instrumentation; Mind is only a middle term of consciousness, the mental being can only be a transitional being. If, then, man is incapable of exceeding mentality he must be surpassed and Supermind and superman must manifest and take the lead of the creation. But if his mind is capable of opening to what exceeds it, then there is no reason why man himself should not arrive at Supermind and supermanhood or at least lend his mentality, life and body to an evolution of that greater term of the Spirit manifesting in Nature.[4]

The ascent of man from the physical to the supermental must open out the possibility of a corresponding ascent in the grades of substance to that ideal or causal body which is proper to our supermental being, and the conquest of the lower principles by Supermind and its liberation of them into a divine life and a divine mentality must also render possible a conquest of our physical limitations by the power and principle of supramental substance. And this means the evolution not only of an untramelled consciousness, a mind and sense not shut up in the walls of the physical ego or limited to the poor basis of knowledge given by the physical organs of sense, but a life-power liberated more and more from its mortal limitations, a physical life fit for a divine inhabitant and — in the sense not of attachment or of restriction to our present corporeal frame but an exceeding of the law of the physical body, — the conquest of death, an early immortality. For from the divine Bliss, the original Delight of existence, the Lord of Immortality comes pouring the wine of that Bliss, the mystic Soma, into these jars of mortalised living matter; eternal and beautiful, he enters into these sheaths of substance for the integral transformation of the being and nature.[5]

The Divine descends from pure existence through the play of Conscious-Force and Bliss and the creative medium of Supermind into cosmic being; we ascend from Matter through a developing life, soul and mind and the illuminating medium of Supermind towards the divine being. The knot of the two, the higher and the lower hemisphere, is where mind and Supermind meet with a veil between them. The rending of the veil is the condition of the divine life in humanity, for by that rending, by the illumining descent of the higher into the nature of the lower being and the forceful ascent of the lower being into the nature of the higher, mind can recover its divine light in the all-comprehending Supermind, the soul realise its divine self in the all-possessing, all-blissful Ananda, life repossess its divine power in the play of omnipotent Conscious-Force and Matter open to its divine liberty as a form of the divine Existence.[6]

The Unknowable knowing itself as Sachchidananda is the one supreme affirmation of Vedanta; it contains all the others or on it they depend . . . The universe and the individual are the two essential appearances into which the Unknowable descends and through which it has to be approached.[7]

We speak of the evolution of Life in Matter, the evolution of Mind in Matter; but evolution is a word which merely states the phenomenon without explaining it. For there seems to be no reason why Life should evolve out of material elements or Mind out of living form, unless we accept the Vedantic solution that Life is already involved in Matter and Mind in Life because in essence Matter is a form of veiled Life, Life a form of veiled Consciousness.[8]

I am seeking to bring some principle of inner Truth, Light, Harmony, Peace into the earth-consciousness; I see it above and know what it is — I feel it ever gleaming down on my consciousness from above and I am seeking to make it possible for it to take up the whole being into its own native power, instead of the nature of man continuing to remain in half-light, half-darkness. I believe the descent of this Truth opening the way to a development of divine consciousness here to be the final sense of the earth evolution.[9]

World and Māyā

Thus not any eternal and original law of eternal and original Matter, but the nature of the action of cosmic Mind is the cause of atomic existence. Matter is a creation, and for its creation the infinitesimal, an extreme fragmentation of the Infinite, was needed as the starting point or basis . . . But this Matter, like Mind and Life, is still Being or Brahman in its self-creative action. It is a form of the force of conscious Being, a form given by Mind and realised by Life.[10]

World is Maya. World is not unreal in the sense that it has no sort of existence; for even if it were only a dream of the Self, still it would exist in It as a dream, real to It in the present even while ultimately unreal. Nor ought we to say that world is unreal in the sense that it has no kind of eternal existence; . . . (it has) an eternal recurrence if not an eternal persistence, an eternal immutability in sum and foundation along with an eternal mutability in aspect and apparition . . .

Still world is Maya because it is not the essential truth of infinite existence, but only a creation of self-conscious being, — not a creation in the void, not a creation in nothing and out of nothing, but in the eternal Truth and out of the eternal Truth of that Self-being . . .[11]

Maya [is] the power of infinite consciousness . . . to form . . . Name and Shape out of the vast illimitable Truth of infinite existence. It is by Maya that static truth of essential being becomes ordered truth of active being, — or, to put it in more metaphysical language, out of the supreme being in which all is all without barrier of separative consciousness emerges the phenomenal being in which all is in each and each is in all for the play of existence with existence, consciousness with consciousness, force with force, delight with delight.[12]

There is . . . a line of reasoning which . . . affirms that the question how the Illusion generated . . . is illegitimate . . . If a real universe does not exist, a cosmic Illusion exists and we are bound to inquire how it came into being or how it manages to exist, what is its relation or non-relation to the Reality, what is meant by our own existence in Maya, by our subjugation to her cycles, by our liberation from her.[13]

But for the Illusionist the individual soul is an illusion and non-existent except in the inexplicable mystery of Maya. Therefore we arrive at the escape of an illusory non-existent soul from an illusory non-existent bondage in an illusory non-existent world as the supreme good which that non-existent soul has to pursue![14]

Supermind, Overmind, Mind

We have started with the assertion of all existence as one Being whose essential nature is Consciousness, one Consciousness whose active nature is Force or Will; and this Being is Delight, the Consciousness is Delight, this Force or Will is Delight . . .

But when we thus assert this unity of Sachchidananda on the one hand and this divided mentality on the other, we posit two opposite entities one of which must be false if the other is to be held as true, one of which must be abolished if the other is to be enjoyed . . . From this solution there is no escape unless there be an intermediate link between the two which can explain them to each other and establish between them such a relation as will make it possible for us to realise the one Existence, Consciousness, Delight in the mould of the mind, life and body.

The intermediate link exists. We call it the Supermind or Truth-Consciousness, because it is a principle superior to mentality and exists, acts and proceeds in the fundamental truth and unity of things and not like the mind in their appearances and phenomenal divisions.[15]

We have to regard therefore this all-containing, all-originating, all-consummating Supermind as the nature of the Divine Being, not indeed in its absolute self-existence, but in its action as the Lord and Creator of its own worlds. This is the truth of that which we call God.[16]

Mind is no independent and original entity but only a final operation of the Truth-Consciousness or Supermind, therefore wherever Mind is, there Supermind must be. Supermind or the Truth Consciousness is the real creative agency of the universal Existence.[17]

We perceive a graduality of ascent, . . . a scale of intensities which can be regarded as so many stairs in the ascension of Mind or in a descent into Mind from That which is beyond it . . . If we accept the Vedic image of the Sun of Truth . . . we may compare the action of the Higher Mind to a composed and steady sunshine, the energy of the Illumined Mind beyond it to an outpouring of massive lightenings of flaming sun-stuff. Still beyond can be met a yet greater power of the Truth-Force, an intimate and exact Truth-vision, Truth-thought, Truth-sense, Truth-feeling, Truth-action, to which we can give in a special sense the name of Intuition . . . At the source of this Intuition we discover a super-conscient cosmic Mind in direct contact with the supramental Truth-Consciousness . . . not Mind as we know it, but an Over-mind that covers as with the wide wings of some creative Oversoul that whole lower hemisphere of Knowledge — Ignorance, links it with that greater Truth-Consciousness while yet at the same time with its brilliant golden lid it veils the face of the greater Truth from our sight . . . This then is the occult link we were looking for; this is the Power that at once connects and divides the supreme Knowledge and the cosmic Ignorance.[18]

The transition to Supermind through Overmind is a passage from Nature as we know it into Supernature. It is by that very fact impossible for any effort of the mere Mind to achieve.

Our first decisive step out of our human intelligence, our normal mentality, is an ascent into a higher Mind, a mind no longer of mingled light and obscurity or half-light, but a large clarity of the Spirit . . . It is . . . a power that has proceeded from the Overmind — but with the Supermind as its ulterior origin . . .[19]

Gnostic Being

As there has been established on earth a mental Consciousness and Power which shapes a race of mental beings and takes up into itself all of earthly nature that is ready for the change, so now there will be established on earth a gnostic Consciousness and Power which will shape a race of gnostic spiritual beings and take up into itself all of earth-nature that is ready for this new transformation.[20]

The gnosis is the effective principle of the Spirit, a highest dynamic of the spiritual existence. The gnostic individual would be the consummation of the spiritual man; his whole way of being, thinking, living, acting would be governed by the power of a vast universal spirituality.[21]

In the gnostic or divine being, in the gnostic life, there will be a close and complete consciousness of the self of others, a consciousness of their mind, life, physical being which are felt as if they were one's own. The gnostic being will act, not out of a surface sentiment of love and sympathy or any similar feeling, but out of this close mutual consciousness, this intimate oneness.[22]

A life of gnostic beings carrying the evolution to a higher supramental status might fitly be characterised as a divine life; for it would be a life in the Divine, a life of the beginnings of a spiritual divine light and power and joy, manifested in material Nature.[23]

But the gnostic soul, the vijñānamaya puruṣa, is the first to participate not only in the freedom, but in the power and sovereignty of the Eternal. For it receives the fullness, it has the sense of plenitude of the Godhead in its action; it shares the free, splendid and royal march of the Infinite, is a vessel of the original knowledge, the immaculate power, the inviolable bliss, transmutes all life into the eternal Light and the eternal Fire and the eternal Wine of the nectar. It possesses the infinite of the Self and it possesses the infinite of Nature.[24]

Self

In relation to the individual the Supreme is our own true and highest self, that which ultimately we are in our essence, that of which we are in our manifested nature. A spiritual knowledge, moved to arrive at the true Self in us, must reject, as the traditional way of knowledge rejects, all misleading appearances.[25]

We have to know ourselves as the self, the spirit, the eternal; we have to exist consciously in our true being. Therefore this must be our primary, if not our first one and all-absorbing idea and effort in the path of knowledge.[26]

Spiritual experience tells us that there is a Reality which supports and pervades all things as the Cosmic Self and Spirit, can be discovered by the individual even here in the terrestrial embodiment as his own self and spirit, and is, at its summits and in its essence, an infinite and eternal Being, Consciousness and Bliss of existence.[27]

Integral Yoga

The complete realisation of unity is therefore the essence of the integral knowledge and of the integral Yoga. To know Sachchidananda one in Himself and one in all His manifestations is the basis of knowledge; to make that vision of oneness real to the consciousness in its status and in its action and to become that by merging the sense of separate individuality in the sense of unity with the Being and with all beings is its effectuation in Yoga of knowledge; to live, think, feel, will and act in that sense of unity is its effectuation in the individual being and the individual life. This realisation of oneness and this practice of oneness in difference is the whole of the Yoga.[28]

Politics and Society

Independence, 14 August 1947

I have been asked for a message on this great occasion, but I am perhaps hardly in a position to give one. All I can do is to make a personal declaration of the aims and ideals conceived in my childhood and youth and now watched in the beginning of fulfilment, because they are relevant to the freedom of India . . . I have always held and said that India was arising, not to serve her own material interests only, to achieve expansion, greatness, power and prosperity, — though these too she must not neglect, — and certainly not like others to acquire domination of other peoples, but to live also for God and the world as a helper and leader of the whole human race. Those aims and ideals were in their natural order these: a revolution which would achieve India's freedom and her unity; the resurgence and liberation of Asia and her return to the great role which she had played in the progress of human civilisation; the rise of a new, a greater, brighter and nobler life for mankind which for its entire realisation would rest outwardly on an international unification of the separate existence of the peoples, preserving and securing their national life but drawing them together into an overriding and consummating oneness; the gift by India of her spiritual knowledge and her means for the spiritualisation of life to the whole race; finally, a new step in the evolution which, by uplifting the consciousness to a higher level, would begin the solution of the many problems of existence which have perplexed and vexed humanity, since men began to think and to dream of individual perfection and a perfect society.[29]

Revolution and Violence

If Sri Aurobindo had not believed in the efficacy of violent revolution or had disliked it, he would not have joined the secret society whose purpose was to prepare a national insurrection . . . In his public activity he took up non-cooperation and passive resistance as a means in the struggle for independence but not the sole means . . .[30]

In some quarters there is the idea that Sri Aurobindo's political standpoint was entirely pacifist, that he was opposed in principle and in practice to all violence and that he denounced terrorism, insurrection, etc., as entirely forbidden by the spirit and letter of the Hindu religion. It is even suggested that he was a forerunner of the gospel of Ahimsa. This is quite incorrect. Sri Aurobindo is neither an impotent moralist not a weak pacifist.[31]

Sri Aurobindo has never concealed his opinion that a nation is entitled to attain its freedom by violence, if it can do so or if there is no other way; whether it should do so or not, depends on what is the best policy, not on ethical considerations of the Gandhian kind.[32]

War

The military necessity, the pressure of war between nations and the need for prevention of war by the assumption of force and authority in the hands of an international body, World-State or Federation or League of Peace, is that which will most directly drive humanity in the end towards some sort of international union.[33]

The elimination of war is one of the cherished ideals and expectations of the age. But what lies at the root of this desire? A greater unity of heart, sympathy, understanding between men and nations, a settled will to get rid of national hatreds, greeds, ambitions, all the fertile seeds of strife and war? If so, it is well with us and success will surely crown our efforts. But of this deeper thing there may be something in sentiment, but there is still very little in action and dominant motive.[34]

Only when man has developed not merely a fellow-feeling with all men, but a dominant sense of unity and commonalty, only when he is aware of them not merely as brothers, — that is a fragile bond — but as parts of himself, only when he has learned to live, not in his separate personal and communal ego-sense, but in a large universal consciousness, can the phenomenon of war, with whatever weapons, pass out of his life without the possibility of return.[35]

Letter to the Governor of Madras covering a contribution to the Viceroy's War Purposes Fund.

We feel that not only is this a battle waged in just self-defence and in defence of the nations threatened with the world-domination of Germany and the Nazi system of life, but that it is a defence of civilisation and its highest attained social, cultural and spiritual values and of the whole future of humanity.[36]

Extracts from a letter written to a disciple in defence of Aurobindo's support of the Allies in the war.

What we say is not that the Allies have not done wrong things, but that they stand on the side of the evolutionary forces . . . The

Divine takes men as they are and uses men as His instruments even if they are not flawless in virtue, angelic, holy and pure . . . Even if I knew that the Allies would misuse their victory or bungle the peace or partially at least spoil the opportunities opened to the human world by that victory, I would still put my force behind them. At any rate things could not be one-hundredth part as bad as they would be under Hitler.[37]

Nationalism and Internationalism

There is a creed in India today which calls itself Nationalism, a creed which has come to you from Bengal. This is a creed which many of you have accepted when you called yourselves Nationalists. Have you realised, have you yet realised, what that means? . . . You call yourselves Nationalists. What is Nationalism? Nationalism is not a mere political program; Nationalism is a religion that has come from God; Nationalism is a creed which you shall have to live. Let no man dare to call himself a Nationalist if he does so merely with a sort of intellectual pride, thinking that he is more patriotic, thinking that he is something higher than those who do not call themselves by that name. If you are going to be a nationalist, if you are going to assent to this religion of Nationalism, you must do it in the religious spirit. You must remember that you are the instruments of God . . . If you have realised that, then you are truly Nationalists; then alone will you be able to restore this great nation.[38]

Internationalism is the attempt of the human mind and life to grow out of the national idea and form and even in a way to destroy it in the interest of the larger synthesis of mankind . . . The height and nobility of the idea is not to be questioned and certainly a mankind which set its life upon this basis would make a better, purer, more peaceful and enlightened race than anything we can hope to have at present. But as the human being is now made, the pure idea, though always a great power, is also afflicted by a great weakness. It has an eventual capacity, once born, of taking hold of the rest of the human being and forcing him in the end to acknowledge its truth and make some kind of attempt to embody it; that is its strength. But also because man at present lives more in the outward than in the inward, is governed principally by his vital existence, sensations, feelings and customary mentality rather than by his higher thought-mind, and feels himself in these to be really alive, really to exist and be, while the world of ideas is to him something remote and abstract and, however powerful and interesting in its way, not a living thing, the pure idea seems, until it is embodied in life, something not quite real; in that abstractness and remoteness lies its weakness.[39]

Social Reform

But you are surely mistaken in thinking that I said that we work spiritually for the relief of the poor. I have never done that. My work is not to intervene in social matters within the frame of the present humanity but to bring down a higher spiritual light and power of a higher character which will make a radical change in the earth-consciousness.[40]

Nation or Society

The nation or society, like the individual, has a body, an organic life, a moral and aesthetic temperament, a developing mind and a soul behind all these signs and powers for the sake of which they exist. One may see that, like the individual, it essentially is a soul rather than has one; it is a group soul that, once having attained to a separate distinctness, must become more and more self-conscious and find itself more and more fully as it develops its corporate action and mentality and its organic self-expressive life.[41]

State

The State tends always to uniformity, because uniformity is easy to it and natural variation is impossible to its essentially mechanical nature; but uniformity is death, not life. A national culture, a national religion, a national education may still be useful things provided they do not interfere with the growth of human solidarity on the one side and individual freedom of thought and conscience and development on the other; for they give form to the communal soul and help it to add its quota to the sum of human advancement; but a State education, a State religion, a State culture are unnatural violences.[42]

NOTES

1   Aurobindo Ghose, *The Life Divine*, (Pondicherry, 1973), Book II, Part II, 662.
2   Ibid., 683.
3   Ibid., 705.
4   Ibid., 846 – 7.
5   Ibid., Book I, Part I, 261.
6   Ibid., 264 – 5.
7   Ibid., 43.
8   Ibid., 3.
9   Aurobindo Ghose, *On Himself*, (Pondicherry, 1972), 143.
10 *The Life Divine*, Book I, Part I, 238 – 9.
11 Ibid., 101 – 2.
12 Ibid., 115.
13 Ibid., Book II, Part I, 447.
14 Ibid., Book I, Part I, 38.
15 Ibid., 142 – 3.
16 Ibid., 132.
17 Ibid., 174.
18 Ibid., 277 – 8.
19 Ibid., Book II, Part II, 921, 939.
20 Ibid., 967.
21 Ibid., 971 – 2.
22 Ibid., 1030.
23 Ibid., 1067.
24 Aurobindo Ghose, *The Synthesis of Yoga*, (Pondicherry, 1971), 480.
25 Ibid., 280.
26 Ibid., 352.
27 Aurobindo Ghose, *The Human Cycle*, (Pondicherry, 1971), 158.
28 *The Synthesis of Yoga*, 402.
29 *On Himself*, 401.
30 Ibid., 17.
31 Ibid., 22.
32 Ibid., 41.
33 *The Human Cycle*, 463.
34 Ibid., 576.
35 Ibid., 587.
36 *On Himself*, 393.
37 Ibid., 394 – 8.
38 Aurobindo Ghose, *Speeches*, 7 – 9.
39 *The Human Cycle*, 525 – 7.
40 *On Himself*, 151.
41 *The Human Cycle*, 29.
42 Ibid., 283.

REFERENCES

Aurobindo Ghose, *The Life Divine*, Book I and Book II, Parts I and II. Pondicherry: Śri Aurobindo Ashram, 1973.

Aurobindo Ghose, *On Himself. Compiled from Notes and Letters.* Pondicherry: Śri Aurobindo Ashram, 1972.

Aurobindo Ghose, *The Human Cycle, the Ideal of Human Unity, War and Self Determination.* Pondicherry: Śri Aurobindo Ashram, 1971.

Aurobindo Ghose, *The Synthesis of Yoga.* Pondicherry: Śri Aurobindo Ashram, 1971.

13

SARVEPALLI RĀDHAKRISHNAN (1888 – 1975)

Born at Tirutani, South India, Rādhakrishnan's early religious training from dedicated parents was strengthened by study at the Lutheran Mission High School at Tirupati (1896 – 1900), Voor-hees' College, Velore (1900 – 1904) and Madras Christian College (1904 – 1908). He felt impelled to study Hindu thought if only to meet the questionings and explicit criticism of the teachers at the Christian institutions he attended of certain aspects of the Indian religious tradition. The need for philosophy, he maintains, comes about when traditional faith is challenged and it is as a philosopher and an interpreter of Hindu thought that he is best known.

His academic career began in 1909 as a philosophy teacher at Presidency College, Madras. There he continued his studies of the Hindu classics and Western philosophical thought. His academic distinctions included the post of Vice-Chancellor of Banares Hindu University and Spalding Professor of Eastern Religions at Oxford University. He was elected Vice-President of India in 1952 and President in 1962, an indication of the high regard in which he was held by his fellow countrymen and a clear recognition of his services to the nation. But his greatest distinction was as an interpreter of Advaita Vedānta and as an exponent of the religion of the spirit.

His writings include volumes on Indian philosophy and religion, the relation of Eastern religion and Western thought, the Hindu and Idealist view of life, and education, politics and soci-ety. Commentating on his interest in philosophy, Rādhakrishnan maintains that it was a cousin's gift of G.F. Stout's *Manual of Psychology*, J. Welton's *Logic* and J.S. MacKenzie's *Manual of Ethics* that determined his choice of philosophy as the primary interest of his life. This fortuitous act as it seemed persuaded him that life was more than a matter of chance and that spiritual forces were at work determining our destiny. His approach to philosophy from the religious rather than the scientific or historical standpoint was determined by his religious upbringing and his interest in the interaction of Eastern and Western thought. He claims that in his philosophical writings he seeks above all to convey his insight into the meaning of life, to provide a coherent and consistent interpretation of the world, and to promote the religion of the spirit.

His spiritual interpretation of the universe sees the cosmic process as a movement with a specific direction and goal. There is no discontinuity between human life and spiritual life any more than there is discontinuity between animal life and human life since all forms of life are an expression of the Divine Spirit. Spiritual life may be regarded as the completion or fulfilment of human life and the goal of the cosmic process is the establishment of a kingdom of free spirits. What this means is that the world is not illusory; it is a manifestation of God or the Divine Spirit and hence real. But its reality is not ultimate or absolute; it is a dependent or created reality which is what the doctrine of māyā seeks to convey. The world depends on the immanent activity of God without which it would cease to be. It is a particular manifestation of divine, creative activity and its dissolution does not affect the absolute reality of God.

Knowledge of the primordial Spirit or the divine source of the universe, according to Rādhakrishnan, is possible as a result of a rational analysis of empirical data but true and certain knowledge comes through an immediate, intuitive apprehension of the nature of ultimate reality. This immediate awareness is spoken of as jñāna, or bodhi, or gnosis, or integral insight. It is a state of ecstasy; it is man's self-fulfilment; it is what is meant by being with God and it is an experience common to all religions.

Rādhakrishnan recognizes the significance of learning about the basic principles of the great religions of the world and sees it as essential to the promotion of international understanding. Where interreligious rivalries prevail there is no possibility of establishing a world community with a world culture. Interreligious understanding involves also the abandonment of missionary activity and proselytizing which presupposes the belief that one religion is superior to another. The aim of religious education should be to enable all believers of whatever creed to learn about the basic principles of their own religions. Each religion takes its own path to the goal of union with the Divine but their unity lies in that which is eternal in them. No one religion can lay claim to being exclusive; religious traditions are imperfect expressions of the immutable essence of religion which is ultimate truth.

Rādhakrishnan's religious philosophy is not without social implications. The belief that all men are bound together in one spirit means that a life of service and sacrifice is inevitable for those who would promote the religion of the spirit. It is man's duty to create and defend institutions that preserve the ideals of freedom, justice and truth and to promote the development of a truly human life. Equally it is man's responsibility to condemn those institutions, like the caste system for example, which degrade and humiliate large sections of society and to show concern for the status of women in society. Rādhakrishnan's claim is that the common aim of religion and philosophy is to preserve those spiritual values which unite mankind.

SARVEPALLI RĀDHAKRISHNAN

Religion

Religion has been identified with feeling, emotion and sentiment, instinct, cult and ritual, perception, belief and faith, and these views are right in what they affirm, though wrong in what they deny. Schleiermacher is not wrong in saying that there is a predominant feeling element in the religious consciousness. Religious feeling, however, is quite distinct from any other kind of feeling. Nor is it to be identified with a sense of creaturely dependence; for then Hegel might retort that Schleiermacher's dog may be more pious than his master. If we assimilate religious experience to the moral consciousness, as Kant is inclined to do, we overlook the distinctive characters of the two activities. Religion is not mere consciousness of value. There is in it a mystical element, an apprehension of the real and an enjoyment of it for its own sake which is absent in the moral consciousness. Religion is not a form of knowledge as Hegel sometimes urged. While religion implies a metaphysical view of the universe, it is not to be confused with philosophy.

All the religions owe their inspiration to the personal insights of their prophet founders. The Hindu religion, for example, is characterized by its adherence to fact. In its pure form, at any rate, it never leaned as heavily as other religions do on authority. It is not a 'founded' religion; nor does it centre round any historical events. Its distinctive characteristic has been its insistence on the inward life of the spirit. To know, possess and be the spirit in this physical form, to convert an obscure plodding mentality into clear spiritual illumination, to build peace and self-existent freedom in the stress of emotional satisfactions and sufferings, to discover and realize the life divine in a body subject to sickness and death has been the constant aim of the Hindu religious endeavour.[1]

Religion in this sense will be a binding force which will deepen the solidarity of human society. The encounter of the different religions has brought up the question whether they could live side by side or whether one of them would supersede the others. Mankind at each period of its history cherishes the illusion of the finality of its existing modes of knowledge. This illusion breeds intolerance and fanaticism. The world has bled and suffered from the disease of dogmatism, of conformity. Those who are conscious of a mission to bring the rest of humanity to their own way of life have been aggressive towards other ways of life. This ambition to make disciples of all nations is not the invention of the Communists. If we look upon our dogmatic formulations as approximations to the truth and not truth itself, then we must be prepared to modify them if we find other propositions which enter deeper into reality. On such a view it will be illogical for us to hold that any system of theology is an official, orthodox, obligatory and final presentation of truth. Reality is larger than any system of theology, however large.[2]

Religion begins for us with an awareness that our life is not of ourselves alone. There is another, greater life enfolding and sustaining us. Religion as man's search for this greater self will not accept any creeds as final or any laws as perfect. It will be evolutionary, moving ever onward. The witness to this spiritual view is borne, not only by the great religious teachers and leaders of mankind, but by the ordinary man in the street, in whose inmost being the well of the spirit is set deep. In our normal experience events happen which imply the existence of a spiritual world. The fact of prayer or meditation, the impulse to seek and appeal to a power beyond our normal self, the moving sense of revelation which the sudden impact of beauty brings, the way in which decisive contacts with certain individuals bring meaning and coherence into our scattered lives, suggest that we are essentially spiritual. To know oneself is to know all we can know. A spiritual as distinct from a dogmatic view of life remains unaffected by the advance of science and criticism of history. Religion generally refers to something external, a system of sanctions and consolations, while spirituality points to the need for knowing and living in the highest self and raising life in all its parts. Spirituality is the core of religion and its inward essence, and mysticism emphasizes this side of religion.[3]

Hinduism

— Hinduism adopts a rationalist attitude in the matter of religion. It tries to study the facts of human life in a scientific spirit, not only the obvious facts, the triumphs and defeats of men who sleep in spiritual unconsciousness, but the facts of life's depths. Religion is not so much a revelation to be attained by us in faith as an effort to unveil the deepest layers of man's being and get into enduring contact with them.

The religions of the world can be distinguished into those which emphasize the object and those which insist on experience. For the first class religion is an attitude of faith and conduct directed to a power without. For the second it is an experience to which the individual attaches supreme value. The Hindu and Buddhist religions are of this class. For them religion is salvation. It is more a transforming experience than a notion of God. Real religion can exist without a definite conception of the deity but not without a distinction between the spiritual and the profane, the sacred and the secular.[4]

There has been no such thing as a uniform stationary unalterable Hinduism whether in point of belief or practice. Hinduism is a movement, not a position; a process not a result; a growing tradition not a fixed revelation.[5]

In religion, Hinduism takes its stand on a life of spirit, and affirms that the theological expressions of religious experience are bound to be varied. One metaphor succeeds another in the history of theology until God is felt as the central reality in the life of man and the world. Hinduism repudiates the belief resulting from a dualistic attitude that the plants in my garden are of God, while those in my neighbour's are weeds planted by the Devil which we should destroy at any cost. On the principle that the best is not the enemy of the good, Hinduism accepts all forms of belief and lifts them to a higher level. The cure for error is not the stake or the cudgel, not force or persecution, but the quiet diffusion of light.[6]

Mission

There are thus three different attitudes, right, centre, and left, which Christian missionaries adopt towards other religions. Here, as elsewhere, the hopes of the future are under the left-wing of liberals and not with the reactionaries or conservatives. If we do not bring together in love those who sincerely believe in God and seek to do His will, if we persist in killing one another theologically, we shall only weaken men's faith in God. If the great religions continue to waste their energies in a fratricidal war instead of looking upon themselves as friendly partners in the supreme task of nourishing the spiritual life of mankind, the swift advance of secular humanism and moral materialism is assured. In a restless and disordered world which is unbelieving to an extent which we have all too little realized, where sinister superstitions are setting forth their rival claims to the allegiance of man, we cannot afford to waver in our determination that the whole of humanity shall remain a united people, where Muslim and Christian, Buddhist and Hindu shall stand together bound by common devotion, not to something behind but to something ahead, not to racial past or a geographical unit, but to a great dream of a world society with a universal religion of which the historical faiths are but branches. We must recognize humbly the partial and defective character of the isolated traditions and seek their source in the generic tradition from which they all have sprung.[7]

The man of faith, whether he be Hindu or Buddhist, Muslim or Christian, has certainty, and yet there is a difference between the two pairs. The attitude of the cultivated Hindu and the Buddhist to other forms of worship is one of sympathy and respect, and not criticism and contempt for their own sake. This friendly understanding is not inconsistent with deep feeling and thought. Faith for the Hindu does not mean dogmatism. He does not smell heresy in those who are not entirely of his mind. It is not devotion that leads to the assertive temper, but limitation of outlook, hardness, and uncharity. While full of unquestioning belief, the Hindu is at the same time devoid of harsh judgement. It is not historically true that in the knowledge of truth there is of necessity great intolerance.[8]

Intuitive Knowledge

There is a knowledge which is different from the conceptual, a knowledge by which we see things as they are, as unique individuals and not as members of a class or units in a crowd. It is non-sensuous, immediate knowledge. Sense knowledge is not the only kind of immediate knowledge. As distinct from sense knowledge or *pratyakṣa* (literally presented to a sense), the Hindu thinkers used the term *aparokṣa* for the non-sensuous immediate knowledge. This intuitive knowledge arises from an intimate fusion of mind with reality. It is knowledge by being and not by sense or by symbols. It is awareness of the truth of things by identity. We become one with the truth, one with the object of knowledge. The object known is seen not as an object outside the self, but as part of the self. What intuition reveals is not so much a doctrine as a consciousness; it is a state of mind and not a definition of the object.[9]

The deepest things of life are known only through intuitive apprehension. We recognize their truth but do not reason about them. In the sphere of values we depend a good deal on this kind of knowledge. Both the recognition and creation of values are due to intuitive thinking. Judgments of fact require dispassionateness; judgments of value depend on vital experience. Whether a plan of action is right or wrong, whether an object presented is beautiful or ugly can be decided only by men whose conscience is educated and whose sensibility is trained. Judgments of fact can be easily verified while value-judgments cannot. Sensitiveness to quality is a function of life, and is not achieved by mere learning. It is depended on the degree of development of the self.[10]

God and the Absolute

While the Absolute is pure consciousness and pure freedom and infinite possibility, it appears to be God from the point of view of the one specific possibility which has become actualized. While God is organically bound up with the universe, the Absolute is not. The world of pure being is not exhausted by the cosmic process which is only one of the ways in which the Absolute reality which transcends the series reveals itself . . .

God is the Absolute from the human end. When we limit down the Absolute to its relation with the actual possibility, the Absolute appears as supreme Wisdom, Love and Goodness. The eternal becomes the first and the last.[11]

The religious devotee envisages the supreme reality in the form of a personal God who is the source, guide and destiny of the world. The difference between the Supreme as absolute Spirit and the Supreme as personal God is one of standpoint and not of essence. It is a difference between God as He is and God as He seems to us. Personality is a symbol, and if we ignore its symbolic character it shuts us out from the truth.[12]

Every belief in Ultimate Reality as God is restrictive in character. It fixes limits, boundaries. The assumption of a personal God as the ground of being and creator of the universe is the first stage of the obscuring and restriction of the vision which immediately perceives the great illumination of Reality. It permits the knowledge of the truth that ever transcends God, does not annihilate God but comprises it.[13]

God and Man

If there is one doctrine more than other which is characteristic of Hindu thought, it is the belief that there is an interior depth to the human soul, which, in its essence, is uncreated and deathless and absolutely real. The spirit in man is different from the individual ego; it is that which animates and exercises the individual, the vast background of his being in which all individuals lie. It is the core of all being, the inner thread by being strung on which the world exists. In the soul of man are conflicting tendencies: the attraction of the infinite, which abides for ever, changeless, unqualified, untouched by the world; and the fascination of the finite, that which like the wind-beaten surface of the waters is never for a moment the same. Every human being is a potential spirit and represents, as has been well said, a hope of God and is not a mere fortuitous concourse of episodes like the changing forms of clouds of the patterns of a kaleidoscope. If the feeling for God were not in man, we could not implant it any more than we could squeeze blood from a stone. The heart of religion is that man truly belongs to another order, and the meaning of man's life is to be found not in this world but in more than historical reality. His highest aim is release from the historical succession denoted by birth and death.[14]

The aim of life is the gradual revelation in our human existence of the eternal in us. The general progress is governed by the law of *Karma* or moral causation. The Hindu religion does not believe in a God who from His judgment-seat weighs each case separately and decides on its merits. He does not administer justice from without, enhancing or remitting punishment according to His sweet will. God is *in* man, and so the law of *Karma* is organic to man's nature. Every moment man is on his trial, and every honest effort will do him good in his eternal endeavour. The character that we build will continue into the future until we realise our oneness with God.[15]

Mokṣa

It is the aim of religion to lift us from our momentary meaningless provincialism to the significance and status of the eternal, to transform the chaos and confusion of life to that pure and immortal essence which is its ideal possibility. If the human mind so changes itself as to be perpetually in the glory of the divine light, if the human emotions transform themselves into the measure and movement of the divine bliss, if human action partakes of the creativity of the divine life, if the human life shares the purity of the divine essence, if only we can support this higher life, the long labour of the cosmic process will receive its crowning justification and the evolution of centuries unfold its profound significance. The divinizing of the life of man in the individual and the race is the dream of the great religions. It is the *mokṣa* of the Hindus, the *nirvāṇa* of the Buddhists, the kingdom of heaven of the Christians. It is for Plato the life of the untroubled perception of the pure idea. It is the realization of one's native form, the restoration of one's integrity of being . . . The world process reaches its consumation when every man knows himself to be immortal spirit, the son of God and is it.[16]

Mokṣa is spiritual realisation. The Hindu Dharma says, Man does not live by bread alone, nor by his work, capital, ambition or power or relation to external nature. He lives or must live by his life of spirit. Mokṣa is self-emancipation, the fulfilment of the spirit in us in the heart of the eternal. This is what gives ultimate satisfaction, and all other activities are directed to the realisation of this end.[17]

Māyā

If we raise the question as to how the finite rises from out of the bosom of the infinite, Śaṁkara says that it is an incomprehensible mystery, māyā. We know that there is the absolute reality, we know that there is the empirical world, we know that the empirical world rests on the Absolute, but the *how* of it is beyond our knowledge. The hypothesis of creation is a weak one, and it assumes that God lived alone for some time and then suddenly it occurred to him to have company when he put forth the world. The theory of manifestation is not more satisfying, for it is difficult to know how the finite can manifest the infinite. If we say that God is transformed into the world, the question arises whether it is the whole of God that is transformed or only a part. If it is the whole, then there is no God beyond the universe and we lapse into the lower pantheism. If it is only a part, then it means that God is capable of being partitioned. We cannot keep one part of God above and another part below. It would be like taking half a fowl for cooking, leaving the other half for laying eggs. Śaṁkara believes that it is not possible to determine logically the relation between God and the world. He asks us to hold fast to both ends. It does not matter if we are not able to find out where they meet.[18]

The view that regards the multiplicity as ultimate is deceptive (māyā), for it causes the desire to live separate and independent lives. When we are under the influence of māyā, we think that we are completely separate entities, sharing little and mistaking individuality, which is one of the conditions of our life in space-time, for isolation and not wishing to lose the hard outlines of our separate existence. Māyā keeps us busy with the world of succession and finitude. It causes a certain restlessness in our soul, fever in our blood. It tempts us to accept, as real, bubbles which will be broken, cobwebs which will be swept away. This wearing of masks, this playing of roles, this marionette performance of ourselves, is mistaken for truth. We forget that we are more closely allied in spirit than we suspect, that we share infinitely more than we realize.[19]

Caste

The institution of caste illustrates the spirit of comprehensive synthesis characteristic of the Hindu mind with its faith in the collaboration of races and the co-operation of cultures. Paradoxical as it may seem, the system of caste is the outcome of tolerance and trust. Though it has now degenerated into an instrument of oppression and intolerance, though it tends to perpetuate inequality and develop the spirit of exclusiveness, these unfortunate effects are not the central motives of the system. If the progressive thinkers of India had the power, as they undoubtedly have the authority, they would transform the institution out of recognition.[20]

Caste, on its racial side, is the affirmation of the infinite diversity of human groups. Though the Vedic Aryans started their life in India with a rigid and narrow outlook, regarding themselves as a sort of chosen people, they soon became universal in intention and developed an ethical code applicable to the whole of humanity, a mānavadharma . . . Indiscriminate racial amalgamation was encouraged by the Hindu thinkers. The Hindu scriptures recognised the rules about food and marriage which the different communities were practising. What we regard as the lower castes have their own taboos and customs, laws and beliefs which they have created for themselves in the course of ages. Every member of the group enters into the possession of the inheritance bequeathed. It is the law of use and want that distinguishes one group from its neighbour. Caste is really custom. Crude and false as the customs and beliefs of others may seem to us, we cannot deny that they help the community adopting them to live at peace with itself and in harmony with others.[21]

Caste as a trade guild is not yet out of date. While the suggestion of a definite programme of life at the very beginning is not undesirable, still stereotyping it without the least regard to the natural endowment and special aptitudes is likely to result in an enslavement of life which finds it difficult to adjust itself to the complex condition of the modern world . . .

People with different racial heritages can live together in amity and friendship only on the basis of caste. The formulators of the institution felt that, though birth was the only available test, spiritual character was the real basis of the divisions of society.[22]

NOTES

1   *An Idealist View of Life*, (London, 1961), 69 – 70.
2   *Indian Religions*, (New Delhi, 1979), 13.
3   *Eastern Religion and Western Thought*, (Oxford, 1940), 61.
4   Ibid., 20 – 1.
5   *The Hindu View of Life*, (London, 1964), 129.
6   Ibid., 125.
7   *Eastern Religions and Western Thought*, 347.
8   Ibid., 314.
9   *An Idealist View of Life*, 108 – 9.
10 Ibid., 112.
11 Ibid., 272 – 3.
12 *Indian Religions*, 102.
13 *Religion in a Changing World*, (London, 1967), 122.

14 *Eastern Religions and Western Thought*, 83.
15 *Indian Religions*, 52 – 3.
16 *An Idealist View of Life*, 97 – 8.
17 *The Hindu View of Life*, 81.
18 Ibid., 66 – 7.
19 *Eastern Religions and Western Thought*, 94 – 5.
20 *The Hindu View of Life*, 93.
21 Ibid., 97 – 9.
22 *Indian Religions*, 85, 87.

REFERENCES

S. Radhakrishnan, *An Idealist View of Life*. London: George Allen and Unwin, 1961.
S. Radhakrishnan, *The Hindu View of Life*, London: George Allen and Unwin, 1964.
S. Radhakrishnan, *Eastern Religions and Western Thought*. Oxford: Oxford University Press, 1940.
S. Radhadrishnan, *Religion in a Changing World*. London: George Allen and Unwin, 1967.
S. Radhakrishnan, *Indian Religions*. New Delhi: Vision Books, 1979.

14

VINOBĀ BHĀVE (1895 – 1983)

Born in 1895 into a comfortable home in Kolaba, Mahārāshtra, Vinobā benefited from the care and attention of a pious mother and the concern of a father that his two sons should be provided with a good education. Vinobā showed great interest in the pursuit of knowledge and wisdom but not in the acquisition of degrees which accounted for his failure to sit his examinations at Bombay University and his deparature for Benares to study Sanskrit. It was there that he first encountered the views of Gandhi whose speech on such themes as the importance of native languages, the plight of the poor as compared with the rich, and the need for cleanliness in personal and public life, filled him with such admiration and enthusiasm that in 1916 he joined Gandhi's ashram at Sabarmati near Ahmedabad.

Vinobā's moral and spirital development at Sabarmati won him the praise and admiration of Gandhi who sent him to Wardha in 1921 to start a new ashram. There he laboured diligently proving himself to be a true disciple of Gandhi and was chosen to be the first satyāgrahi when the civil disobedience movement began.

His years in prison as a result of the satyāgraha campaigns were put to good use by his study of the languages of South India, and after Gandhi's death the movement turned to him among others for leadership and inspiration. His response was to inaugurate the bhūdān movement in 1951 in the Nalgonda district of Telengana. The purpose of the movement was to encourage wealthy landowners to donate voluntarily land to those who had none. He saw this as a possible solution to the poverty of India and in six years he succeeded in acquiring four million acres of land for distribution by the bhūdān movement. The parallels between Vinobā's movement and Gandhi's doctrine of trusteeship according to which the rich are persuaded to part voluntarily with their surplus wealth for the benefit of the poor is evident. The emphasis in both instances is on persuasion rather than coercion, a concept firmly rejected by both as contrary to the principle of ahiṁsā.

A further response on Vinobā's part was to insist that ahiṁsā implied the establishment of lok-niti — government by the people, rather than rāj-niti — government by politicians. This in turn involved the decentralization of government and the development of self-sufficient, self-governing village units. Gramrāj, village government, was a form of swarāj with each village having the power to manage its own affairs. This meant the progressive abolition of government control and the creation of a stateless society. But it did not mean accepting the necessity of a totalitarian dictatorship as an intermediate stage as the communists claimed. For Vinobā the best government is no government at all, or freedom from government. This was what he meant by sarvodaya.

With the decentralization of government and the development of gramrāj went the responsibility of educating the people to manage their own affairs. Vinobā's concept of Nai Talim — new education, involved the introduction of a programme directed to establishing a vidyapith, a seat of knowledge or university in each village, in order to preserve the unity of the village by providing a complete education for all who required it. It involved also recognition of the principle of social equality which meant acknowledging the need for equitable distribution of land, the establishing of village industries, and the abolition of waste. In short his new education programme was education for life.

While many parallels exist between Vinobā and Gandhi as might be expected given their close relationship, Vinobā developed this theories in his own way and the Bhūdān movement might be regarded as his distinctive contribution to the problem of the poverty of India.

VINOBĀ BHĀVE

Sarvodaya

Sarvodaya does not mean good government or majority rule, it means freedom from government, it means decentralisation of power. We want to do away with government by politicians and replace it by a government of the people, based on love, compassion and equality. Decisions should be taken, not by a majority, but by unanimous consent; and they should be carried out by the united strength of the ordinary people of the village[1]

I am continually urging that believers in non-violence should use their strength to establish *lok-niti* — government by the people: in other words, to put an end to *raj-niti* — government by politicians. 'Raj' and 'niti' are words which embody mutually contradictory ideas, they cancel each other out. Where *niti*, the moral law, rules, government disintegrates; where there is *raj*, a coercive government, *niti* is destroyed. For the future, we want not a *kingdom*, ruled by political 'kings', but a *common*-wealth, ordered by the 'common' people.[2]

The ultimate goal of sarvodaya is freedom from government . . . A society free from government does not mean a society without order. It means an orderly society, but one in which administrative authority rests in the villages.[3]

In the Sarvodaya structure every village would have its *gram panchayat*,[4] and the *gram panchayat* would have the right to choose its representatives in the state government. Effective power would rest in the *gram panchayat*, and the higher authorities would have only secondary power.[5]

The moral and material welfare of the country will only be assured by the establishment of a band of workers who will keep clear of the whirligig of office, who will be alert and watchful, conscientious in their study of facts, and ready for sacrifice. To such a group we have given the name Sarvodaya Samaj. Sarvodaya is not a seat; it has not compulsory practices, no rigid discipline. Sarvodaya depends upon service through understanding in a spirit of love.[6]

Non-Violence

Now I would like to see a 'Shanti Sena'[7] set up by the people of every village. This body would be active always in service to the people, but it would also be a Shanti Sena to protect and defend the village. This Shanti Sena would derive its strength from the universal consent of the people; without the backing of all of you it would not be able to work.[8]

If we consider that it is right to use violent methods, it follows that the assassin who killed Gandhiji was a man who deserves our respect, even though his ideas may have been mistaken. If you believe that it is right to use violent means to achieve good ends, you must recognise that Gandhiji's murderer also made a great sacrifice. I must tell you plainly that if we as a nation accept the idea that well-meaning people may use violence in order to put their ideas into practice, India will be broken into fragments, and will lose all her strength.[9]

People imagine that *ahimsa* means that we should go to work as cautiously as a man who has a boil or some other injury on his hand, and wants to avoid making it ache by any sudden exertion. Let there be no painful, sudden changes, we say — and so *ahimsa* is rendered innocuous . . . It is therefore very dangerous when people think that non-violence should move slowly; it turns *ahimsa* into a conservative force, a preserver of the *status quo*.[10]

Satyāgraha

Satyagraha for us is a sacred watchword, and one which we believe has power to save the world . . . Men have got it into their heads that *satyagraha* is a negative thing, a method of forcing an issue or exercising pressure which is of very doubtful propriety . . . But where there is *satyagraha*, where we undertake that aspect of *satyagraha* which consists in explaining the idea of *gramdan*[11] to the people, we cannot brook one iota of coercion.[12]

Satyagraha means basing one's whole life on faith in truth, it means holding fast to what we believe to be true no matter what difficulties come, and being willing to endure suffering for it . . .

The road will certainly have its ups and downs. Nevertheless the people must possess the strength to stand fast in the truth in spite of all obstacles. This is the one power that can save the world from violence, and it is the power that can solve the problems of every society. Our education ought to aim at awakening in our students the spirit of *satyagraha*.[13]

Education

Every village should have its *vidyapith*;[14] there shall be a university in every village — that is real *gramraj* . . . You should think twice before you do anything to break up the unity of the village. There is no meaning in giving four years of education in the village and then requiring children to go elsewhere if they want to go further. I ought to be able to get a complete education in my own village, for my village is not a fragment, it is an integral whole.[15]

The spiritual principle of Nai Talim[16] is that knowledge and work are not two things but one. It is a mistake to say that knowledge is higher than work or work than knowledge. Nai Talim is education based on the unity of knowledge and work. In such an education, no one feels that he is being forced to work . . .

The social principle of Nai Talim is that all human lives are equally to be respected. All the various social and class divisions are therefore forms of falsehood. Once this is admitted, our present political and other divisions will be done away with. Social cleavages cannot exist where the principle of Nai Talim is at work. The basis of Bhoodan is the contention that the land is for all, and that no individual ought to exercise rights of ownership in it. If this idea is extended to the international field, it means that no one nation can regard its land as the property of that nation alone. The whole of the land of the world is for the whole of humanity . . .

Nai Talim teachers must consider it a part of their work to do away with inequalities in the village. In every country in the world it is the teachers who have led revolutions. Here too it is an integral part of the work of Nai Talim to change, to revolutionise, the present condition of the villages and establish economic and social equality. We have a four-fold programme including village industries, the equitable distribution of land, the destruction of waste and sectarian barriers and the education for life which is called Nai Talim.[17]

This Nai Talim sets up new standards of value. The old education teaches that it is wrong to steal. The new education teaches that it is equally wrong for a man to accumulate more goods than he needs. The old education assigns different values to bodily and to mental labour. The new education not only regards both as of equal value, it integrates them both into one whole, and makes use of both as a unity. The old education honours ability; the new education considers ability to be the handmaid of equality. The old education honours Lakshmi, Shakti, and Saraswati as three separate divinities.[18] The new education places humanity upon the throne of honour, and considers these three merely as the instruments whereby humanity is to be served.[19]

My own point of view is that true religious teaching is not a matter of literature. The essence of religion is a sound character, faith in God, and the conviction that the soul is other than the body. This essential religion can only be learned from the company of good men. My only plan for religious teaching, therefore, is to choose good men as teachers.[20]

Someone asks: 'What is the purpose of music and art in education?' I reply: 'God is revealed in the world through Name and Form; all else in the Godhead is unembodied. Let His Name be sung in music, and His Form be glorified in art.'[21]

It seems to me that education must be of such a quality that it will train students in intellectual self-reliance and make them independent thinkers. If this were to become the chief aim of learning, the whole process of learning would be transformed.[22]

The most important thing for any kind of education, whether in school or in society, is to bring about the recognition that we are other than our bodies. It is this self-knowledge which is the foundation on which the power of *satyagraha* can be built.[23]

Religion

The strongest institutions in the world today are of two types: religious and governmental. Both have as their objective public service. Society felt the need for both types and is still using them . . .

But as things are today it is necessary that society should be set free from both these types of institution. I do not mean that we need to get rid of religion; that is *not* what I am saying. What I do say is that we need to get rid of religious institutions.[24]

When we look around us today, what do we see to be the condition in the world of religion? There are four major religions,

Islam, Christianity, Hinduism and Buddhism, and there are others not so widespread. All these religions have their own institutions . . . All these religions proclaim their faith in non-violence, peace and love; yet, as you may plainly see, none of their religious institutions is exercising its influence for the establishment of peace . . . These institutions, in fact, exercise no real influence on the daily life of society; but if that were all, no great harm would be done. Their continued existence is, however, in my opinion extremely harmful . . . They promote the idea that certain religious duties ought to be carried out by priests, and that once priests have been set apart for this purpose, the laymen have no further responsibility.[25]

Politics and Economics

Government

The best kind of government is one where it is possible to doubt whether any government exists at all.[26]

The government of a democracy can be compared to a cipher. The cipher has no value of its own. If it follows the figure one, we get 10; if it follows a 2, we get 20; if it follows a 3, we get 30. But the power to make ten, twenty or thirty is not in the cipher. It is you who make use of it, and create a 10 or a 20; it has no independent value. In a democracy the people are everything and the government nothing.[27]

We believe in a stateless society as our ultimate goal. We recognise that in the preliminary stages a certain measure of government is necessary, but we do not agree that it will continue to be necessary at a later stage. Neither do we agree that totalitarian dictatorship is necessary to ensure progress towards a stateless society. On the contrary, we propose to proceed by decentralising administration and authority. In the final stage there would be no coercion but a purely moral authority.[28]

The phrase 'the purification of politics' really means that lok-niti[29] must take the place of power-politics, no matter how long it may take to bring this about. I can see no other way to purify politics in this age of science except by establishing lok-niti. The centralisation of power means that we have democracy only in name, and not in reality. Democracy is committing suicide everywhere, and the only remedy is to bring lok-niti into being.[30]

Decentralization

We hold that the centralisation of the whole, or the greater part, of the government system, makes its subsequent dissolution more difficult. We must therefore start at once to introduce decentralisation, and this will be the basis of all our planning. I do not insist that every village should immediately produce all its own needs. The unit for self-sufficiency may be a group of villages. In short, all our planning will be directed towards a progressive abolition of government control by means of regional self-reliance.[31]

This 'welfare state' involves giving a great deal of power to a few individuals, who will then control the whole life of the people. Plans for all our half-million villages are to be made in Delhi. Decisions which touch every side of our daily lives are to be taken in Delhi. Delhi will decide what social reforms should be undertaken, what wedding laws should be made, how untouchability is to be ended, what system of medicine we are to adopt, what language we are to use, what kind of cinema shows we are to see! If we hand over all this power to the Centre, the people will lose their independence and self-reliance of spirit; and for that reason the power of Delhi ought to be reduced.[32]

The government will never be able to give its intelligent attention, like some four-faced Brahma, to every point of the compass at once. However intelligent it might be, it could not control and plan all the affairs of every village so as to promote the welfare of all. Instead of 'national planning' there must be village planning. I used the word 'instead', but it would be better to say that national planning really means village planning. Delhi should give this village planning whatever outside help is needed. This distribution and decentralisation of authority is the second point of our programme. All that we do tends in that direction, and that is why we want the villages themselves to undertake the redistribution of land.[33]

I tell the village people that if they want to see conditions in the villages improve they will have to gird up their loins and get to work themselves. If anyone has no land, they themselves must see that he is given his share of the village land. They must set up industries. They must decide not to buy any more cloth from outside but to spin and weave all they need themselves. None of this work can be done by government laws. Some people ask why I should have to work for Bhoodan,[34] why government could not distribute land. But if the government were to do it, it would be an act of Delhi *raj*, not a step towards *gramraj*.[35] When we are hungry it is we who must eat, no one else can eat on our behalf. In the same way if we want *gramraj* we ourselves must share the land, no one can do it for us.[36]

Swarāj

It is one mark of swaraj not to allow any outside power in the world to exercise control over oneself. And the second mark of swaraj is not to exercise power over any other. These two things together make swaraj — no submission and no exploitation. This cannot be brought into being by government decree, but only by a revolution in the people's ways of thought.[37]

The meaning of swaraj for the nation as a whole is that no other country should exercise power within our borders. But when *swaraj* becomes a reality in each individual village, we call it *gramraj*. When all the people of a village have reached maturity of judgement, and there is never any need to coerce anyone, that is *Ramraj*.[38]

We want every village to have *swaraj* — to manage its own affairs. We want to see all power vested in the village, so that the job of the State Government will not be to give orders to the village, but instead to keep the villages in touch with one another . . .

Our government ought to be a federation linking together all of our four lakhs of villages. Every village would manage its own affairs according to its own rights, the centre would only offer advice which the villagers would be free to accept or not.[39]

What we need to prepare for, then, is not merely good government but self-government. Self government has two aspects: (i) authority must be decentralised, every village must have full power to manage its own affairs, (ii) through education, philosophy and psychology, men must be taught to honour and respect the strength of love and non-violence, and to pay no respect whatever to violence.[40]

NOTES

1 Vinoba Bhave, *Democratic Values and the Practice of Citizenship*, (Varanasi, 1962), 3.
2 Ibid., 15.
3 Ibid., 25.
4 gram panchayat: village council of elders.
5 *Democratic Values*, 107.
6 Ibid., 202 – 3.
7 Shanti Sena: Peace Army.
8 *Democratic Values*, 121.
9 Ibid., 135.
10 Ibid., 149, 151.
11 gramdam: village-gift; the radical development of bhūdān (land gift) in which villagers give up private property in land and administer the village as a family unit.
12 *Democratic Values*, 152 – 3, 156.
13 Vinoba Bhave, *Thoughts on Education*, (Varanasi, 1959), 250.
14 vidyapith: 'seat of knowledge'.
15 *Democratic Values*, 99.
16 Nai Talim: new education, education for life.
17 *Thoughts on Education*, 72 – 4, 78.
18 i.e. Wealth, Power and Learning.
19 *Thoughts on Education*, 234.
20 Ibid., 117.
21 Ibid., 145.
22 Ibid., 27.
23 Ibid., 252.
24 *Democratic Values*, 7.
25 Ibid., 177 – 8.
26 Ibid., 16.
27 Ibid., 20.
28 Ibid., 29.
29 lok-niti: 'politics of the people'.
30 *Democratic Values*, 54 – 5.
31 Ibid., 30.
32 Ibid., 78 – 9.
33 Ibid., 109.
34 Bhoodan: land gift.
35 gramraj: village government.
36 *Democratic Values*, 101 – 2.
37 Ibid., 13 – 14.
38 Ibid., 98. Ramraj: the ideal society, kingdom of God.
39 Ibid., 105 – 6.
40 Ibid., 118.

REFERENCES

Vinoba Bhave, *Democratic Values and the Practice of Citizenship, Selections from the Addresses of Vinoba Bhave 1951 – 1968.* Translated by Marjorie Sykes. Varanasi: Sarva Seva Sangh Prakashan Kashi, Rajghat, 1962.

Vinoba Bhave, *Thoughts on Education.* Varanasi: Akhil Bharat Sarva Seva Sangh Rajghat, Kashi, 1959.

INDEX